DISCOVER THE AMAZING WORLD OF ANIMALS

Contents

Building Homes

Many animals build homes to raise a family in. These houses are usually made of wood, mud, or stones. They shelter the animals from bad weather and from enemies. Animals can rest, eat, and store food in their houses as well. Some animals build a new home each year. Others keep the same home for most of their lives. Homes are built in all kinds of different places, under the ground, under water, and sometimes up in trees.

Why do beavers build dams?

Before they can build their house, beavers make a lake to put it in. First, they stop a stream from flowing by blocking it with trees and branches. The water cannot flow past this dam so it overflows and makes a lake. The beavers then build their house (called a lodge) in the lake using branches, twigs, mud, and stones. The entrances are under the water so enemies, such as wolves, cannot get inside.

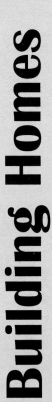

How does a bird build a nest?

Some birds build their nests from twigs, others use grass or even animal hair. The male weaver bird makes his nest from grass. First he hangs a thick piece of grass in a tree and ties a knot to make a loop.

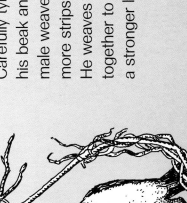

Carefully tying knots using his beak and his feet, the male weaver then adds more strips of grass. He weaves them together to make a stronger loop.

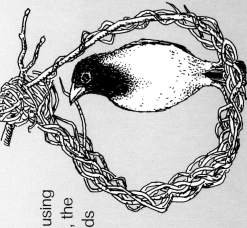

Do baby animals make homes?

Some baby animals have to. If you look into a pond in summer, you may see what look like stones crawling along the bottom. These are the tube-shaped houses of caddisfly larvae, the young of the caddisfly. These larvae make their homes from leaves, sticks, or pebbles which they glue together with a slimy liquid. The head and legs of the caddisfly larva poke out at one end.

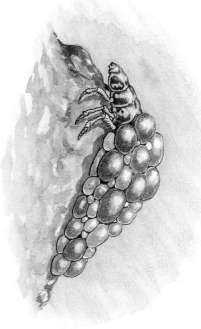

Who lives in a mobile home?

A snail does! In fact, a snail takes its house wherever it goes. This house is the snail's shell. As the animal grows, so the shell grows too.

The snail can pull itself inside its shell and seal up the doorway. This keeps out enemies. It can also help the snail to stay cool and moist in hot weather.

Which bird builds the biggest nest?

Eagles build the biggest nests of any bird, perching them high on a cliff ledge or in a tall tree. The nests, called eyries, are huge piles of sticks and twigs. A mother and father eagle may have several eyries. Each year they choose one to live in, then add more twigs to make it bigger and stronger. Some eyries are as large as a small car!

The weaver bird continues to add more strips of grass, weaving and knotting carefully.

After much hard work the nest takes shape, forming a hollow woven ball.

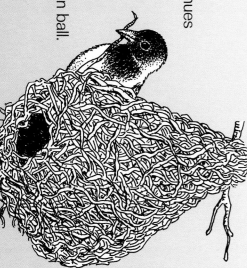

Finally, the nest is ready. The weaver bird leaves a small hole at the bottom of the nest, as an entrance. Having a small, hidden door helps keep out enemies.

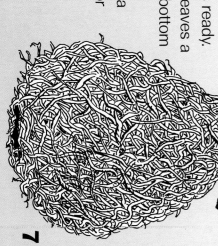

Changing Shape

Human babies look like little adults, but many baby bugs don't look anything like their parents. As some bugs grow up, their bodies change shape. Insects start life as tiny eggs. An egg hatches into the next stage—a larva. Larvae spend nearly all their lives eating, growing, shedding their skins (molting), and then eating some more. Some larvae, like fly maggots, look very different from their parents. They change their shape again to become adults. Other types of bug larvae, such as baby crickets, look more like their parents.

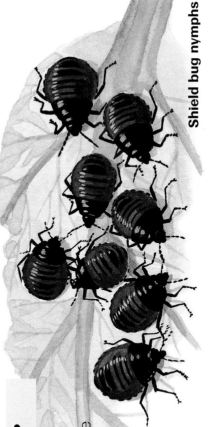

Adult shield bug

Shield bug nymphs

What do baby flies look like?

Baby flies are white wiggly larvae, usually called maggots. These greenbottle larvae look nothing like their parents. They do nothing but eat moldy meat, molt, and grow. Each larva then turns into a pupa—a hard, protective case with the larva inside. The body of the larva breaks down and changes into an adult. When the pupa breaks open, the fly crawls out and flies off.

Which baby insects look like their parents?

Many baby insects, such as shield bugs, grasshoppers, and crickets, look quite like mini-adults. These babies are called nymphs. Shield bug nymphs, however, have no wings. As the nymph grows, it sheds its hard skin. The new skin is soft and allows the body to grow before the skin hardens again. Each time it molts, a nymph grows more like an adult.

What do baby bugs eat?

The brown hawker dragonfly nymph lives in water. It creeps toward a little fish, then shoots forward a hinged flap, or mask. The mask has sharp fangs to stab the fish.

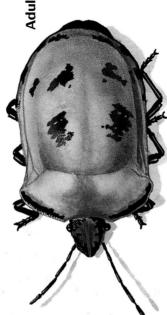

Honeybee larvae have a sweet diet. Worker bees in the hive collect nectar and pollen each day. This is used to make the honey that the larvae are fed on.

How do caterpillars turn into butterflies?

These pictures show the stages in the life of a swallowtail butterfly.

1. The adult butterfly lays her eggs on a leaf. The egg is the first stage of a butterfly's life.

2. The egg hatches into a caterpillar, or larva. The caterpillar spends its life eating leaves. It eats, molts, and grows. The young caterpillar changes its shape and color as it grows.

1. Egg

2. Young caterpillar

Older caterpillar

3. The caterpillar turns into a pupa, or chrysalis. Inside the hard case, the body parts move around and change shape.

4. The chrysalis splits open and the adult butterfly crawls out. It spreads its wings to dry, then flies off to find a mate. This complete change of body shape is called metamorphosis.

4. Adult butterfly

3. Pupa or chrysalis

Other insects that go through these four stages include moths, beetles, flies, bees, wasps, and ants.

The great diving beetle larva lives in fresh water. It stabs small animals like tadpoles with its fangs and injects them with juices. These break down the body into a thick soup.

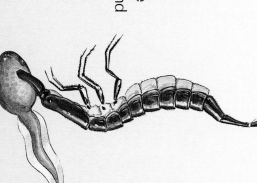

The codling moth larva has strong, sharp jaws. But it doesn't use them to slice up meat. Instead, this hungry caterpillar munches its way through even the hardest apples.

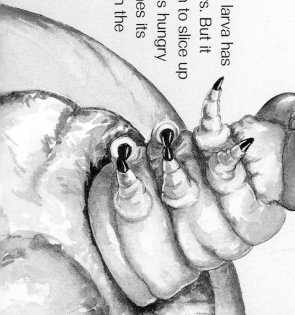

Under Water

Lots of animals live in or under water. These animals, just like all land animals including you, need oxygen to live. Oxygen is an invisible gas. Your body needs oxygen to make it work. Oxygen helps to free the energy in the food that you have eaten and digested. All animals need energy to live, grow, and move about. Land animals get oxygen by breathing air into their lungs or similar body parts. Oxygen is also found in water. Water animals can take in this oxygen through their gills or similar body parts.

How do dolphins breathe?

Dolphins are mammals, like you. So they have warm blood, and lungs for breathing air. If kept under water, they would drown. A dolphin comes to the surface and breathes air through a blowhole on the top of its head.

Is a seahorse an underwater horse?

No, a seahorse is a fish. But it looks a bit like a horse. It has a horse-shaped head but a curly tail to grip seaweed or rocks. Like all fish, it has gills for breathing under the water. These are just behind its eyes. Water comes in through its mouth and flows over its gills. The gills take oxygen from the water into its body. Water flows out through gill slits on the sides of its head.

Who lives on the seashore?

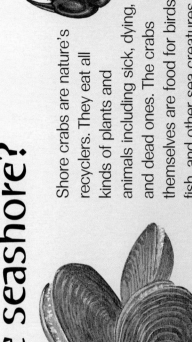

Shore crabs are nature's recyclers. They eat all kinds of plants and animals including sick, dying, and dead ones. The crabs themselves are food for birds, fish, and other sea creatures.

Many creatures that live in rock pools, like these mussels, have shells to protect their soft bodies. Mussels fix themselves to a rock by stringy threads so the waves cannot knock them off. They filter the sea water for food.

Can fish suffocate under the water?

If a fish's gills are blocked it will suffocate. Like all fish, the great white shark has gills on either side of its head. The shark swims along with its mouth wide open. Water flows into its mouth, over the gills, and out through the row of gill slits on its "neck". Except, that is, when the shark bites, and its mouth is full of food. It has to swallow the food quickly, or it will suffocate.

Which animals hold their breath?

Many animals hold their breath under water. Reptiles have lungs and breathe air just like birds and mammals. The green turtle is a reptile which lives in the sea. It needs to come to the surface of the water to get fresh supplies of air. But turtles can hold their breath for much longer than people can. The green turtle can stay under the water for as long as an hour between breaths.

Do only fish have gills?

No, many other water creatures, besides fish, have gills for taking in oxygen from the water. An octopus has gills in the lower part of its "head", which is really its whole body. The gills and other body parts are covered by a large, cloak-shaped flap of skin called the mantle.

Shore fish, like this rock goby, have to cope with being stranded as the tide goes out. The goby has thick, slippery skin and strong, spiny fins. It can skip and slither across the rocks to reach the water.

Oystercatchers have long legs to wade through the water and long beaks to probe in the sand for oysters, mussels, and other shellfish. They peck a hole in the shells and eat the soft flesh inside.

11

Fossil Clues

Dinosaurs lived on Earth millions of years ago, long before people existed. We only know about them from the clues they left behind. When a dinosaur died, the soft parts of its body soon rotted away. The hard parts, such as bones, teeth, and claws, lasted longer. Some dinosaur remains have been preserved in rocks for millions of years. Over that time they have turned into stone. We call these stones fossils. Experts, called paleontologists, dig up these fossils and use them to find out about dinosaurs. They can work out what a dinosaur looked like and how it lived.

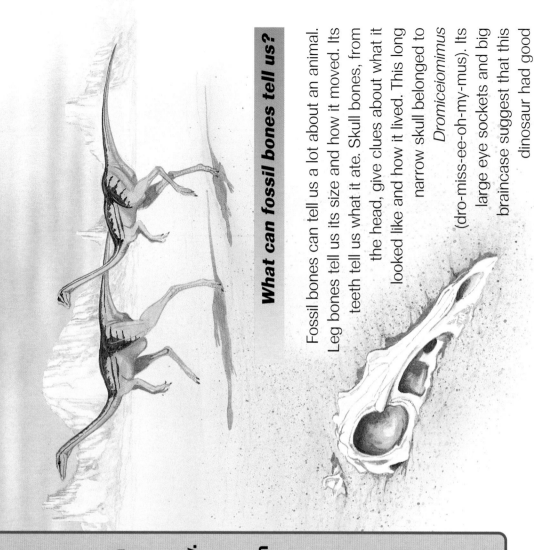

Have dinosaur teeth been found?

Yes, teeth are very hard and tough so they don't rot away easily. This means they often get preserved as fossils. Fossil teeth can give us lots of clues about an animal. The shape, size, and cutting edge of a tooth can tell us how a dinosaur lived and what it ate. *Heterodontosaurus* (het-er-oh-dont-oh-saw-rus) had teeth of different shapes. This means it probably ate lots of different foods. This was unusual for a dinosaur.

What can fossil bones tell us?

Fossil bones can tell us a lot about an animal. Leg bones tell us its size and how it moved. Its teeth tell us what it ate. Skull bones, from the head, give clues about what it looked like and how it lived. This long narrow skull belonged to *Dromiceiomimus* (dro-miss-ee-oh-my-mus). Its large eye sockets and big braincase suggest that this dinosaur had good eyesight and was clever.

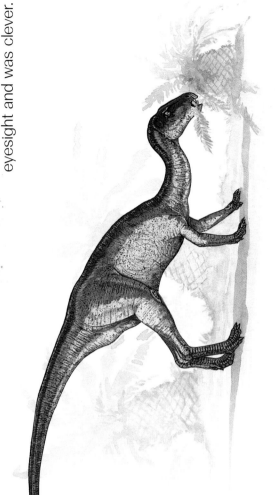

How are fossils formed?

1. When this dinosaur died in a flood, its body sank to the bottom of the riverbed. It lay there, in the mud, for many years.

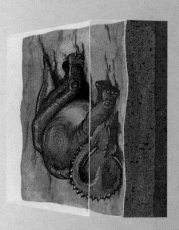

2. Slowly the soft parts of the dinosaur, such as the flesh, rotted away. The body became buried under layers of mud.

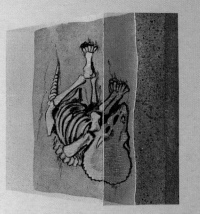

What do fossilized claws tell us?

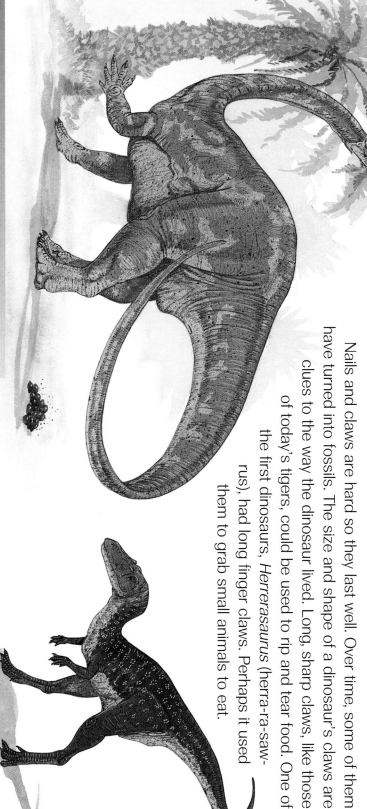

Nails and claws are hard so they last well. Over time, some of them have turned into fossils. The size and shape of a dinosaur's claws are clues to the way the dinosaur lived. Long, sharp claws, like those of today's tigers, could be used to rip and tear food. One of the first dinosaurs, *Herrerasaurus* (herra-ra-saw-rus), had long finger claws. Perhaps it used them to grab small animals to eat.

What kinds of fossil have been found?

Most fossils are bones and teeth, but other types of fossilized remains have been found as well. Fossil eggs, footprints, and bits of scaly skin have been dug up. Sometimes even droppings became fossilized. Animal dung contains bits and pieces of food, so scientists can tell what food the dinosaur ate. Giant dinosaurs such as *Riojasaurus* (ree-ok-a-saw-rus) must have left huge mounds of dung. Luckily, after millions of years, the dung has turned to stone so it doesn't smell!

Did dinosaurs leave footprints?

Yes, when dinosaurs walked on soft mud or sand, they left deep footprints. Sometimes these became hard and turned into fossils. These footprints can give us clues to a dinosaur's size and weight. Some dinosaurs, such as *Camarasaurus* (kam-ar-a-saw-rus), left lots of tracks as they walked along together. This shows that they lived in groups, or herds.

3. Over millions of years the mud and bones turned into rock. The fossil dinosaur skeleton became buried beneath layers of rock.

4. Some fossils are revealed as the layers of rock are slowly worn away. Others are found when experts look for them and dig them up.

13

Animal Cities

Lots of creatures live together in large groups, just as people live together in towns and cities. Usually animals that live together are good neighbors and they all work for the benefit of the whole town. They collect and store food, build, and look after homes, find new partners, raise their families, and chase away enemies. But, just as in the towns and cities where people live, sometimes the animals get into arguments and even fights.

How do wasps build a city?

A wasps' nest is about the size of a basketball with about 1,000 wasps inside. Wasps build the nest from paper that they make from wood. First they scrape up tiny bits of wood with their jaws. Then they chew it into a sticky liquid. Finally, the wasps spread out this liquid, which hardens to make the papery nest walls. Wasps build their nest cities inside a roof or hollow tree.

On the grasslands of North America, small heads sometimes pop out of holes in mounds of earth. These heads belong to prairie dogs. These animals make dog-like barks, but they are really a type of squirrel. More than 10,000 prairie dogs may live in one underground township. Each prairie dog family has its own entrance hole to its own burrows. Prairie dog sentries guard all the burrows and bark a warning if there is danger.

Do all animals live with their families?

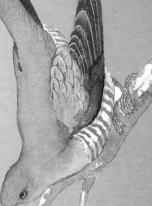

Cuckoos live alone and don't look after their eggs. The female cuckoo lays each of her eggs in the nest of another bird. The cuckoo chick is then raised by foster parents!

Not all animals live in family groups. Lionfish live alone. Their colorful stripes warn other creatures to stay away. The spines of the lionfish are highly venomous.

14

Who builds colonies by the sea?

Puffins, tubby sea birds with big heads and colorful beaks, nest together in "towns", called colonies, along the seashore. Here, most puffin parents dig a burrow for their eggs. Others take over a spare rabbit hole or a tunnel left by another sea bird. Puffin colonies are always noisy places, full of activity.

Do animals build skyscrapers?

Yes—termite mounds can be twice as tall as you and house over a million insects! Termites are tiny, soft insects. They live together in very large groups. Their cities, called termite mounds, have more inhabitants than any others in the animal world. Inside these giant heaps of hard mud and earth, there are many tunnels and chambers. Here the termites are safe from enemies.

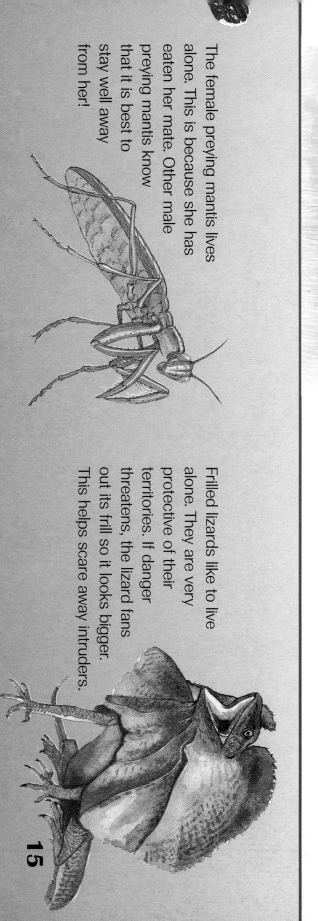

The female preying mantis lives alone. This is because she has eaten her mate. Other male preying mantis know that it is best to stay well away from her!

Frilled lizards like to live alone. They are very protective of their territories. If danger threatens, the lizard fans out its frill so it looks bigger. This helps scare away intruders.

15

Staying Small

Creepy crawlies—insects, spiders, and other minibeasts—are small compared with most other animals. There are lots of reasons for this. Creepy crawlies don't have backbones to support their bodies, like humans do. So the bodies of many minibeasts are covered by a hard outer casing that acts like an outside skeleton, to support and protect them. If a bug got too big, this casing would become too heavy for it to move. Also, bugs don't have lungs. They breathe through air tubes that go from the surface of their body to the inside. If these tubes were too long, fresh air would not flow in fast enough. A giant bug would have difficulty breathing. There are also many advantages to being small.

What is the smallest insect?

One of the tiniest insects is the fairy fly wasp. It is so small that it would fit inside this "o". It looks more like a fly than a wasp. Being this small does have some problems. A fairy fly wasp can't fight its enemies— they're all bigger than it is. But it can hide in tiny cracks where predators can't reach!

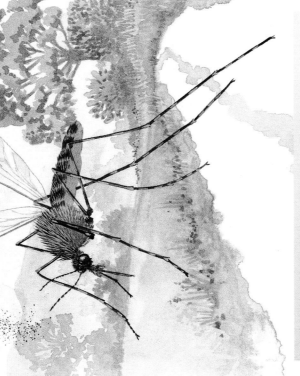

Why is it better to be small?

One reason that bugs stay small is so that they can move around easily to find food. They also need less food than large animals. This means lots of creepy crawlies can live together in one place. This makes finding a mate and breeding easier, too. Midges are tiny flies. Thousands of them fly in a swarm, courting and mating in the air. Some feed on plant juices but others bite animals and suck their blood. They'll even have a meal on you if they get the chance!

Were there prehistoric creepy crawlies?

Yes, the first creepy crawlies left the seas to live on land about 500 million years ago, long before dinosaurs existed. *Meganeura*, a huge dragonfly, lived 270 million years ago. It hunted other flying bugs for food.

Arthropleura was a giant 6ft (1.8m) long armored millipede. It also lived about 270 million years ago and was one of the biggest creepy crawlies ever to walk on Earth.

The Goliath beetle from the tropical rain forests of Africa is about 4¼ inches (over 100mm) long. That's about as big as an insect can grow. Its thick outer casing is like armor, making the Goliath beetle the heaviest insect at about 3½ ounces (100gm)—about the weight of an apple. If it were any larger, the Goliath beetle wouldn't be able to move.

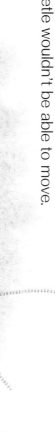

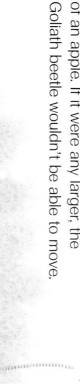

Do bugs live on each other?

Yes, bugs like these tiny mites can live almost anywhere. Mites have eight legs and belong to the same group of animals as spiders. There are thousands of different kinds of mite. Some stab plant stems and suck up the juices, called sap. Others live and feed on animals, biting them and sucking up their blood. The two red mites here are small enough to hitch a ride on a spider's leg.

Do adult moths and butterflies grow?

No, adult moths and butterflies do all their growing when they are caterpillars. As a caterpillar grows, it sheds its skin. The soft skin underneath, which fits its new, bigger body, slowly hardens. A caterpillar may shed its skin several times before it is fully grown. This elephant hawk moth is one of the largest flying insects. Each of its wings is almost 2¾ inches (70mm) across—that's about the width of your hand.

Scorpions were probably some of the first minibeasts on land. Fossils have been found that are five times as big as the largest scorpion alive today. The prehistoric scorpion shown here—*Gigantoscorpion*—was 2ft (60cm) long.

The first spiders lived about 370 million years ago. *Arthrolycosa* was a large spider with long legs. It had special fangs that it probably used to poison its prey.

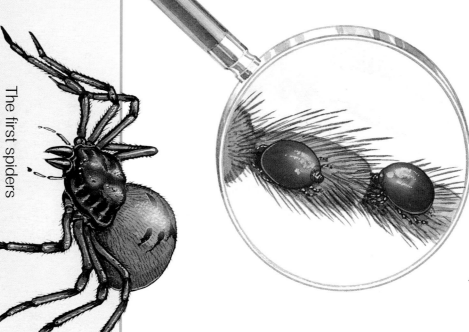

17

Thirst Beaters

Animals need water to stay alive. No creature can survive without it. But not all animals need to drink water. Some can get the water they need from their food. This might be the watery saps and juices in plant food, or the blood and body fluids in animal food. Many desert animals get water in this way. They also lose very little water from their bodies, in their sweat, urine, and droppings. However, when they do find a pool, these animals will drink as much water as they can.

When do camels drink?

Camels do not need to drink very often, but when they do drink, they drink a lot! When a camel finds water, at a well or in the pool of an oasis, it can drink 160 quarts (150 litres) in five minutes. That's almost two bathtubs-full in one go! The camel is well adapted for life in the hot, dry desert in other ways as well. Thick fur protects it from the heat and sunburn, wide feet stop it from sinking into the soft sand, and long eyelashes keep windblown sand out of its eyes.

How do desert animals save water?

The fennec fox is the world's smallest fox. It is about the size of a pet cat and it lives in the Sahara and Arabian deserts. Like many desert animals, it saves as much of its body water as possible. It produces little urine, and its faeces, or droppings, are dry and hard. The fox's huge ears also help it to lose extra body heat, and so stay cool.

How long do animals live?

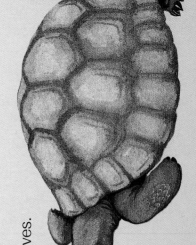

Not all animals live as long as people do but there are some that live longer. One type of clam, an ocean quahog, is thought to live for up to 225 years!

Tortoises also have long lives. Many different kinds of tortoise are thought to live over 100 years. It is possible that they live for even longer.

18

Do all birds drink water?

Not all birds get their water by drinking it. Ostriches live in the grasslands and semi-desert areas of Africa. They eat leaves, shoots, flowers, and seeds, and get the fluid they need from their food. Ostriches can survive most conditions, as long as there are enough plants to eat.

Can animals dig for water?

Yes, some animals do, like the Arabian oryx that lives in the deserts of the Middle East. In the heat of the day, this small antelope finds shade under acacia trees. It scrapes the dry soil with its hooves to uncover food and moisture. In the night, when it is cooler, the oryx walks up to 18 miles (30km) to find new feeding places.

Can animals collect water?

Some creatures can collect water. The thorny devil lives in the desert regions of Australia. During the cool night, dew forms on the ground and on the thorny devil's skin. A network of small grooves on the lizard's skin funnel the moisture to the lizard's mouth.

Which animals drink mist?

The Namib desert in southwest Africa is near the coast. Fog and mist blow in from the sea. The Namib desert beetle gets a drink by standing, head down, on a sand dune. Then misty moisture droplets from the sea can roll down its body into its mouth.

Many animals have very short lives compared to humans. Some live for less than a day. Many types of butterfly only live for one or two weeks.

Small wild birds usually only live for a few years. Larger birds sometimes live for up to 30 years. Parrots are thought to be the longest lived birds. One pet cockatoo was over 80 when it died.

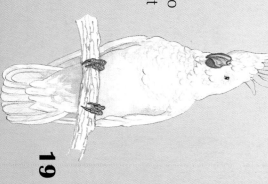

Dinosaur Sizes

Dinosaurs lived on Earth for 160 million years. During that time many different types of dinosaurs lived and died out. They came in all shapes and sizes. Some dinosaurs were huge. Others were small—the size of a chicken today. The largest dinosaurs were the plant-eating sauropods. Some of them were as tall as a four-story building. Dinosaurs were the biggest land animals that have ever lived on Earth.

Were dinosaurs as tall as trees?

Sauropods had huge barrel-shaped bodies, short legs, whiplike tails, and long necks. If they reared up, their long necks could reach to over 65ft (20m). They would have towered over many trees. The longest dinosaur may have been *Seismosaurus* (size-mo-saw-rus). An adult was over 130ft (40m) long—about as long as 10 cars lined up nose to tail.

Were all dinosaurs giants?

No, many dinosaurs were quite small. *Saltopus* (salt-oh-pus), one of the smallest found, was about the size of a chicken. This speedy hunter was so quick it could catch flying insects and fast-moving lizards. *Saltopus's* small size meant that it could hide from its enemies easily. Also, being small meant it needed less food than bigger dinosaurs.

Which are the biggest and tallest animals?

Animals come in all shapes and sizes. The biggest animal that has ever lived is the blue whale. Blue whales can reach lengths of over 100ft (30m). They can weigh up to 130 tonnes—that's the combined weight of about 2,000 men! The biggest animal that lives on land today is the African elephant. These elephants can grow up to 12ft (4m) tall at the shoulder, weighing up to 12 tonnes. The tallest animal alive today is the giraffe. With their long necks, giraffes can be 18ft (6m) tall. Millions of years ago, land animals were much bigger. Many dinosaurs, such as *Tyrannosaurus rex*, were bigger than elephants.

Which dinosaur had the biggest head?

Torosaurus (tor-oh-saw-rus) had the biggest head of any known dinosaur. This large plant-eater was as long as an elephant and weighed as much as five rhinoceroses. Its huge skull bones and the large frill over its neck were the size of a big dining-room table!

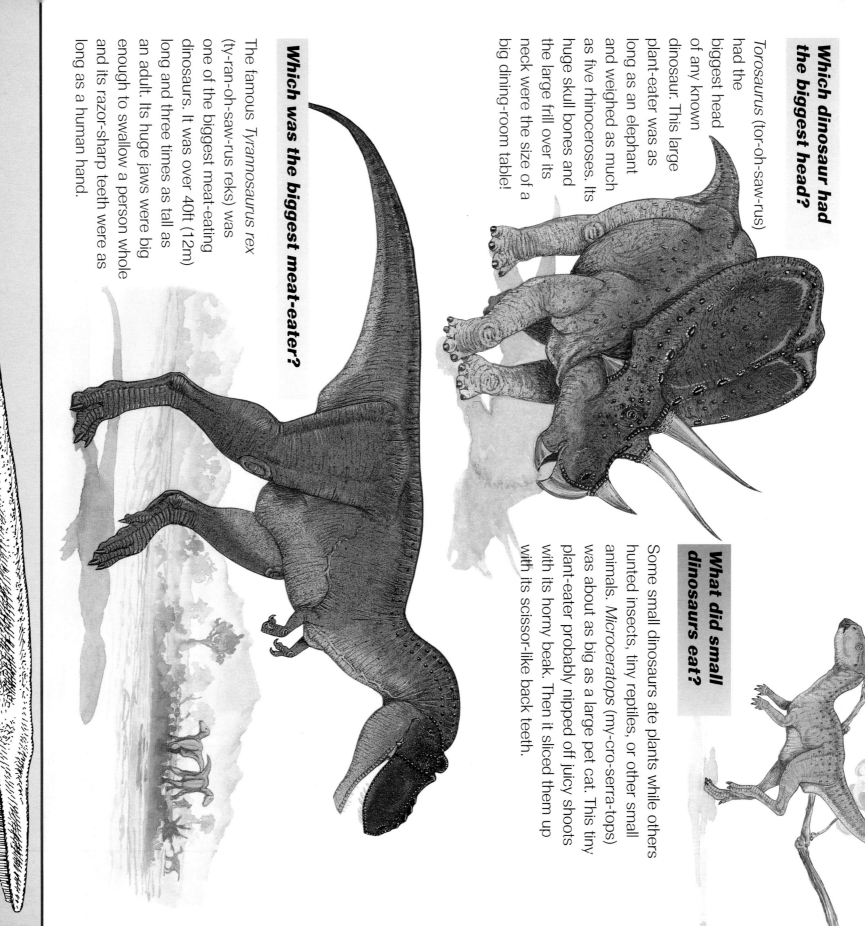

What did small dinosaurs eat?

Some small dinosaurs ate plants while others hunted insects, tiny reptiles, or other small animals. *Microceratops* (my-cro-serra-tops) was about as big as a large pet cat. This tiny plant-eater probably nipped off juicy shoots with its horny beak. Then it sliced them up with its scissor-like back teeth.

Which was the biggest meat-eater?

The famous *Tyrannosaurus rex* (ty-ran-oh-saw-rus reks) was one of the biggest meat-eating dinosaurs. It was over 40ft (12m) long and three times as tall as an adult. Its huge jaws were big enough to swallow a person whole and its razor-sharp teeth were as long as a human hand.

21

Learning Lessons

Many animals are born tiny and helpless. They can do almost nothing except eat, sleep, and grow. As animals get older, they have to learn all kinds of important skills, such as how to hunt for food and how to escape from danger. Some animals learn from their parents. Others, like bugs, know what to do from the day they are born. This knowledge is called instinct.

Are animal parents good teachers?

Chimpanzee parents are very good teachers. Here a young chimp is learning to poke a stick into the nest of small insects called termites. He pulls out the stick and licks off the juicy termites. Chimpanzees learn how to do this from their parents and other group members. They may also discover how to use leaves and stones as tools.

How do animals smell a trail?

These babies are called processionary moth caterpillars because they walk in a long line, called a procession. The leading caterpillar makes sure no one gets lost by leaving a trail of smelly liquid along the branches. So these caterpillars just have to follow their noses!

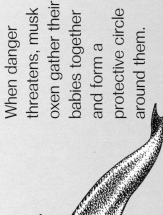

How do animals keep their babies safe?

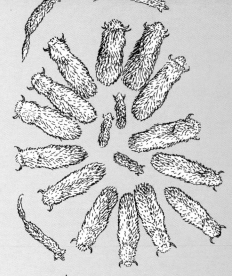

When danger threatens, musk oxen gather their babies together and form a protective circle around them.

Many animals take good care of their babies. When a baby dolphin is born, other dolphins help it stay at the surface of the water so it can breathe. They help the baby until it is able to support itself.

Do animals do chores?

Honey bees have lots of chores to do. First, they learn to clean out their hive. Then they practice flapping their wings and blowing air around the hive to keep it cool. Finally, they discover how to collect sweet, sticky nectar from flowers.

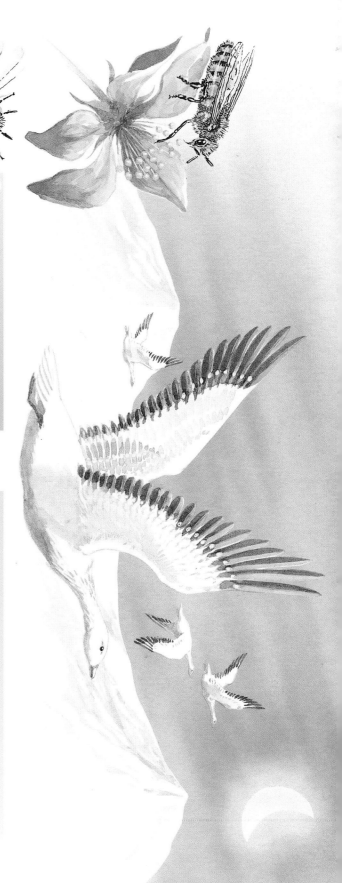

Is there an animal flying school?

Some birds, such as snow geese, go to flying school. Each year, the adults fly north to build nests and have their young. Then, before the winter, they fly back south. The young birds follow the older ones who have made the journey before. The youngsters learn to recognize the rivers, mountains, coastlines, islands, and other places they pass on their trip. Soon they are able to find the way on their own.

Who has swimming lessons?

Baby otters have fun splashing around in rivers, playing with sticks and stones. But they are actually learning to be champion swimmers. They need to dart through the water to catch fresh fish. If they don't work hard, they will end up with nothing for dinner.

A baby deer has a spotted coat to help it stay hidden in the undergrowth. The baby waits quietly while its mother looks for food.

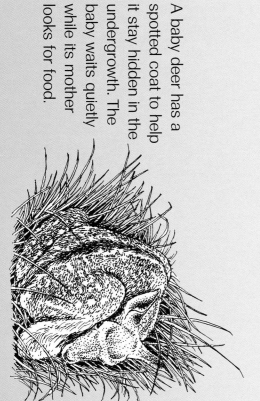

The female sloth keeps her baby safe by taking it with her wherever she goes. The baby hangs on to its mother's belly while she climbs through the trees.

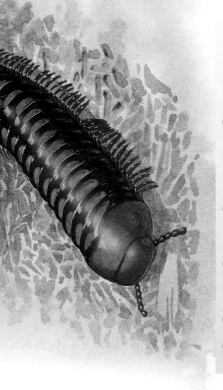

Mini Movers

Since life began on Earth, millions of years ago, many kinds of minibeast have developed. They all have different body shapes, and different types and numbers of legs. Each group of animals is suited to the place it lives in and the kind of life it leads. Insects, such as flies, have six legs. Arachnids, such as spiders, have eight legs. Centipedes and millipedes have lots of legs. Slugs, worms, and snails have none!

How many legs do insects have?

All insects have six legs, but the legs and the insects come in many different shapes and sizes. This bull ant is a big, fierce ant and can be up to an inch (2.5cm) long. Bull ants have strong, biting mouthparts. They guard their nest and larvae and, if an enemy attacks, they bite it and squirt stinging acid. Bull ants will also hunt down and kill insects bigger than themselves to eat.

Which minibeast has most legs?

Millipedes have more legs than most other minibeasts. The name millipede means "thousand-legged". But even this giant millipede does not have that many! Most millipedes have between 100 and 400 legs. They have four legs on each part, or segment, of their bodies. Even though millipedes have lots of legs, they move quite slowly. They walk by lifting up groups of legs at a time. Some legs are swinging forward while others are moving backward. Each foot touches the ground just before the one in front in a wavelike movement.

How do worms move without legs?

An earthworm's body is divided into tiny sections, called segments. Each segment has special hairs to help the worm grip the soil. At rest, a worm's segments are all the same size.

1. To move forward, the hairs on the worm's back end grip the soil. Then the worm stretches its front end forward as far as it can go. These front segments become long and thin.

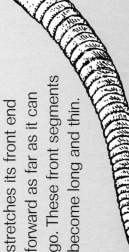

24

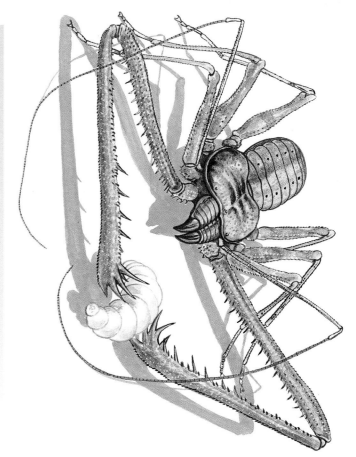

Are legs always used for walking?

Like all scorpions, the tail-less whip scorpion has eight legs. But it only uses six legs for walking. The front pair of legs are much longer and thinner. They are feelers which the scorpion uses to find its way by touch. The whip scorpion also has two huge, powerful pincers in front of its feeler legs. It uses these pincers to grab its prey.

Do centipedes have 100 legs?

Centipedes can have between 30 and 354 legs. They have one pair of legs for each part, or segment, of their bodies. Unlike plant-eating millipedes, centipedes are fierce hunters. This cave centipede uses its long legs to race after its prey. It also uses them to feel its way around the dark caves where it lives. A centipede can even bite with its clawlike front legs!

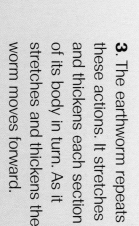

2. Next, the worm stops stretching, and the front section thickens again. The back hairs unhook, and the front hairs grip the soil. The next section then stretches, pulling the back end forward.

3. The earthworm repeats these actions. It stretches and thickens each section of its body in turn. As it stretches and thickens the worm moves forward.

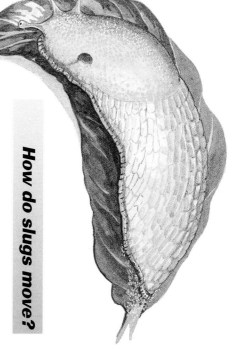

How do slugs move?

Snails and slugs, like this orange-colored great black slug, belong to a group of animals called mollusks. They do not have legs for walking, but they do have a foot! This foot is the flat, slimy base of the animal's body. It is made up of one big muscle. Wavelike ripples pass down the foot muscle from front to back. These movements pull the slug forward over a trail of slippery slime.

Dinosaur Eggs

Dinosaurs belonged to a group of animals called reptiles. Most living reptiles, such as crocodiles, turtles, snakes, and lizards, lay eggs which hatch into young. For a long time experts thought that dinosaurs probably laid eggs too, but no one knew for sure. Then, in 1922, a nest of fossil dinosaur eggs, laid millions of years before, was found. This proved that dinosaurs laid their eggs on land. Later, experts found nests containing fossils of newly hatched young, and eggs with babies still inside.

Where were dinosaur eggs first found?

The first dinosaur eggs were found in 1922, in the Gobi Desert in Mongolia. The eggs belonged to *Protoceratops* (pro-toh-serra-tops), a dinosaur that lived around 100 million years ago. The female *Protoceratops* scraped a nest hole in the ground for her eggs. As many as 30 eggs were found in one nest. The fossil eggs, each about the size of a tennis ball, were arranged in a neat spiral. Some experts think that two or more females laid their eggs in the same nest.

How big were dinosaur eggs?

Dinosaur eggs varied in size, depending on the size of the adults. But even the largest dinosaurs laid relatively small eggs. Some of the largest known dinosaur eggs, about 12 inches (30cm) long, were laid by 40ft (12m) long *Hypselosaurus* (hip-sel-o-saw-rus). A female *Maiasaura* (my-a-saw-ra) was about the size of a big bus but each of her eggs was only the size of a large ostrich egg. Groups of *Maiasaura* nested together. Their huge nesting sites covered whole hillsides.

Did dinosaurs build nests?

Many dinosaurs did build nests to lay their eggs in. All the females in a herd of *Maiasaura* built their nests close together. This helped protect the nests from enemies.

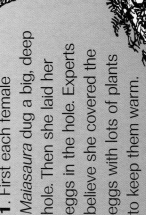

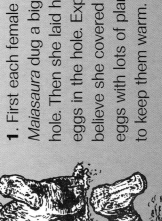

1. First each female *Maiasaura* dug a big, deep hole. Then she laid her eggs in the hole. Experts believe she covered the eggs with lots of plants to keep them warm.

26

Did dinosaurs protect their young?

No one knows for sure, but some dinosaurs may have protected their young. An adult *Styracosaurus* (sty-rak-oh-saw-rus) was longer than two small cars. It was protected by long, sharp horns on its nose and neck frill. But, like all young animals, its babies were at risk from hungry meat-eaters. If attacked, the adult *Styracosaurus* may have formed a circle around their young, like musk oxen do today. The adults' horns would have pointed out toward the enemy, forming a spiny wall. The young stayed safely in the center.

Eggs make a tasty meal for many animals. Dinosaur eggs were good food too, and dinosaurs probably ate each other's eggs. *Oviraptor* (ohv-ih-rap-tor) was a wolf-size dinosaur that could dart along at up to 30 miles (48km) an hour. It lived at the same time as *Protoceratops*. Perhaps it stole eggs from *Protoceratops'* nests. It may have cracked open the shells with its strong fingers.

2. The female *Maiasaura* watched over her nest. She had to guard against greedy egg thieves and make sure that her eggs stayed warm and protected in the nest.

3. After several weeks the eggs began to crack and the baby *Maiasaura* hatched out. To begin with, the hatchlings were fed and cared for by their mother.

27

Living Underground

Some animals live almost their entire lives under the ground. They eat, rest, feed, and breed in their dark world. Other animals make tunnels and burrows for shelter. These creatures usually come out into the open air to find food and a mate. But they sleep and raise their families underground. Some animals make their homes deep in dark holes and caves. These underground homes are usually safe from the animal's enemies. They also shelter the creature from bad weather.

Are animals active all year round?

No, some animals spend a long time in a deep sleep called hibernation. North American groundhogs, or woodchucks, spend half the year inside their burrow in hibernation. They sleep all through the winter when food is hard to find.

Are underground homes easy to spot?

Some underground homes are very easy to see. Moles live in tunnels under the ground, which may total 650ft (200m) in length. When a mole digs a new tunnel, it leaves the earth it has excavated on the surface in a pile that we call a molehill. Moles usually eat tiny creatures they find in their tunnels. After rain, a mole will sometimes venture to the surface in search of worms.

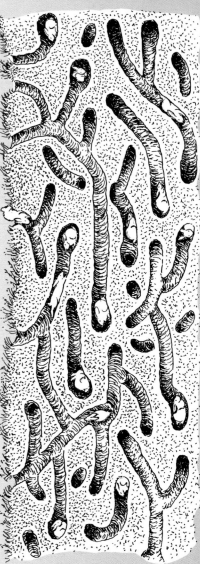

What does a rabbit warren look like inside?

No two rabbit warrens look the same. Each warren has a maze of twisting tunnels and several entrances. A rabbit warren is not all built at once. Each new generation of rabbits adds to it and the warren grows. Some warrens have existed for hundreds of years.

28

How do animals make underground homes?

Animals that make burrows and holes usually have body parts that are specially adapted for digging. The spadefoot toad has a flattened side on each back foot, like a tiny shovel. The toad can dig itself straight down into loose soil and disappear in less than 20 seconds!

Do animals ever share their homes?

Yes, some do. The tuatara, a type of reptile from New Zealand, lives on a few rocky islands off the coast. This strange creature lives in a burrow which it often shares with a petrel or other sea bird. The tuatara goes out at night to hunt for spiders and beetles, and the bird goes in for a night's rest!

Do all birds make their nests in trees?

Although most birds like to make their homes in trees, not all do. Burrowing owls live in dry grasslands where there are no trees. So these small owls shelter and raise their chicks in a burrow. But they don't dig the burrow. They use an empty one, or they borrow or steal a ready-made burrow from another animal.

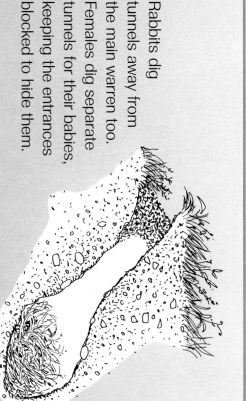

Rabbits dig tunnels away from the main warren. Females dig separate tunnels for their babies, keeping the entrances blocked to hide them.

Rabbits make sure they have special escape holes in the warren. That way, while an enemy is lost in the maze of passages, the rabbits can get out quickly.

29

Minibeast Meals

All animals need to eat to stay alive. Some bugs are hunters, catching and killing other animals for their food. Others feed on plants. Most minibeasts have mouths for eating and drinking. They don't have teeth in their mouths like you, but they do have mouthparts. The way a bug's mouthparts look and work depends on the food it eats. Some creepy crawlies have sharp, cutting mouthparts for biting and tearing their food. Others have sucking mouthparts to drink a liquid meal.

Proboscis coiled for flying

Proboscis uncoiled for feeding

What do butterflies eat?

Butterflies, like these red admirals, drink nectar from flowers. A butterfly's mouthparts are shaped like a drinking straw called a proboscis. It sucks up the thick, sugary liquid through the hollow tube, just like you suck up a milk shake. When a butterfly is not feeding, its proboscis is coiled up under its head. Moths feed in the same way.

Do spiders have teeth?

Spiders have two sharp fangs to stab and kill their prey. The trap-door spider's fangs are huge. The fangs are fixed the spider's tiny mouth which is just behind the fangs. A hole leads from the mouth to each fang. When a spider catches its prey, it stabs it with its fangs. Venom flows through the holes into the fangs and is injected into the prey. Juices in the venom break down the body of the victim. Most spiders then suck up their food, like sucking thick soup through a straw.

Fangs

How do spiders catch their food?

Many spiders make webs of silk to catch their prey.
1. First, the spider fastens one end of its silk to a twig. Then it lets the breeze blow the silk onto another twig to make a bridge.

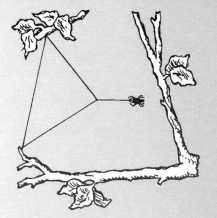

2. The spider makes a loop of silk below the bridge. From the middle of the loop it spins a shorter loop and drops to form a "Y" shape. At the bottom, the spider fastens the silk.

How do flies feed?

Flies, such as this bluebottle, have mouthparts shaped like a sponge on a stalk. When a fly lands on food, it drips juices from its mouth onto the food. These juices break the food down into a thin, runny liquid. Then the fly uses its spongy mouthparts to mop up its soupy food.

Can beetles eat wood?

Even though wood is tough, some minibeasts, like the death watch beetle, make a meal of it. This beetle has mouthparts like powerful pincers. Its strong jaws move these pincers from side to side to shred the wood into bits. The beetle bores through the solid wood until it comes out of a small hole. The male also uses its strong jaws to tap on the wood to attract a mate.

Do bugs eat plants?

Lots of creepy crawlies feed on the leaves, stems, flowers, and roots of plants. Many bugs, like these aphids, feed on plant sap. Sap is a sweet liquid, full of goodness. It runs through tiny tubes inside a plant's stems, stalks, and leaves. The aphid pierces the plant with its hollow, needlelike mouthparts and sucks up the sap.

3. Next, the spider goes back to the center of the web. It spins several more lines to make a framework between the twigs and leaves. These strands are made of nonsticky silk.

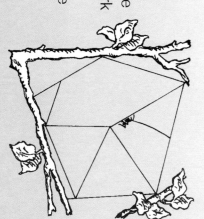

4. The spider spins more threads out from the center like the spokes of a wheel. Then it spins a spiral of sticky threads around the web. This sticky spiral will catch tiny animals.

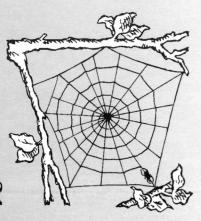

Storing Food

Animals don't have refrigerators to keep their food in. But many creatures do store their food in special hiding places. That way they can make sure they have enough food to eat all year round. In late summer, the trees are covered with fruits, nuts, and berries. So animals get to work collecting, burying, and storing the food. Then, when winter comes, and food is in short supply, the animals can collect food from their stores.

Do animals eat all the food they hide?

Animals don't always find all the food they have buried and stored. When nuts are ripe, a squirrel rushes about gathering the nuts and burying them here, there, and everywhere. During the winter, when the trees are bare, the squirrel sniffs and digs, and finds perhaps half of the nuts it hid. The other nuts are not all wasted. Some grow into new trees.

Do animals eat their leftovers?

Some do. A crocodile sometimes catches a zebra or an antelope. This is far too big for one meal. So the crocodile eats as much as it can, then pushes the leftovers under a rock or log in the river. The meat stays safely in place and softens in the warm water. A few days later, the croc comes back for a second helping.

Where do animals sleep?

Other animals don't stop what they are doing when they need to sleep. The swift goes on very long journeys. It doesn't take a break to sleep, it sleeps as it flies!

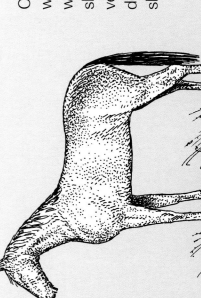

Many animals don't have beds to sleep in and some don't even lie down. Horses sleep standing up. They lock their knees so they don't fall over.

Which creature eats frozen food?

The Arctic fox scrapes a hole and buries its food in the frozen ground, just like you use a freezer. But the fox does not have a microwave oven or cooker to thaw its meal of Arctic hare, lemming, or small bird. It simply digs up the food, then waits until the frozen meal melts in its mouth.

Why store dung?

If some animals didn't eat droppings and dung the world would be full of it. The favorite food of the dung beetle is warm, moist, freshly produced dung. The beetle rolls dung up in a ball, lays its eggs in it, and hides the ball in a burrow. When the eggs hatch, the beetle grubs have their food waiting. For the grubs, the stored dung is just like living in a larder.

Which bird keeps a meat larder?

The shrike is a fierce hunter of insects, small lizards, frogs, mice, and other little creatures. On a good day, it catches more victims than it can eat. So it sticks the extra ones onto thorns or plant spines to save for later. This gruesome larder is what has given the shrike its other name—the butcher bird.

Some animals do have beds to sleep in though, particularly domestic animals. This little kitten likes to curl up in its cosy little bed to go to sleep—just like you!

In order to breathe, sharks need water to pass through their mouth and over their gills. This means they have to keep swimming, even when they are fast asleep.

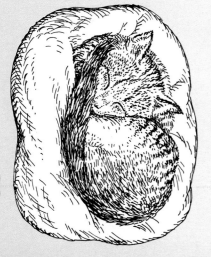

33

Spots and Stripes

Many animals have amazing patterns on their coats with all sorts of different spots and stripes. Some of these colored patterns help the animals to blend in with their background. This kind of disguise is called camouflage. Camouflage helps an animal to hide and survive. A hunter that cannot easily be seen can creep up unnoticed on its prey. The camouflaged prey can more easily hide from the hunter! Some other animals use their bold, bright coats to make them look scary and frighten their enemies away.

How do spots help animals hide?

Spots can be a great camouflage. The pampas cat lives in the grasslands, scrub, and forests of South America. This medium-size cat creeps through the dark night, hunting for mice and other small mammals, and for insects, birds, lizards, and their eggs. The cat's dark spots help to disguise its body shape in the shadows of the moonlit undergrowth. A pet tabby cat is blotched and striped for the same reason.

Why is a zebra stripy?

Few animals are as striped as a zebra. This close relation of the horse has dark brown stripes on a white background—or is it the other way round? Zebras live in groups, or herds, on the savannahs of Africa. The zebras' stripes help to protect them from hungry predators. When zebras spot danger, they run. A hunter, such as a lion, has great trouble picking out one victim from the flashing, dazzling mass of moving stripes.

Which are the fastest animals on land?

The cheetah is the fastest animal on land. It can reach speeds of more than 60 miles (100km) per hour when chasing its prey. Cheetahs can only run that fast for short distances though and they soon need to rest.

The ostrich is the largest bird in the world. It can't fly but it can run extremely fast! An adult ostrich uses its powerful legs to escape from danger at up to 45 miles (70km) per hour.

Are all spots and stripes for camouflage?

Some animals have glaring spots or stripes which are not for camouflage. Instead of helping the animal to hide, they show up clearly. The ladybug's bright patterns are called warning colors. They warn other animals that a ladybug tastes horrible. Birds and other animals soon learn this, and they leave ladybugs alone.

Do any animals have spots and stripes?

Hyenas have spots and stripes, but not on the same animal. The striped hyenas (shown here) live in northern Africa, the Middle East, and India. The spotted hyena has spots instead of stripes. It lives in the grasslands of east and southern Africa. Both types of hyena are fierce hunters and scavengers. Their patterns are mainly for camouflage. They help the hyenas blend in among the dry grasses.

Do all animals need camouflage?

Some creatures are so huge and strong that they do not need a disguise or camouflage. The rhinoceros is the world's second biggest land animal, and it is a very plain colour. Its main defences are size, weight, a very thick skin, and a sharp nose horn. Hardly any predators dare to attack it. If they do, they get speared by its horn and trampled under its massive body.

The pronghorn antelope cannot run as fast as a cheetah but it can keep going for longer. It can race along at 35 miles (55km) per hour for 15 minutes and has a top speed of 55 miles (88km) per hour.

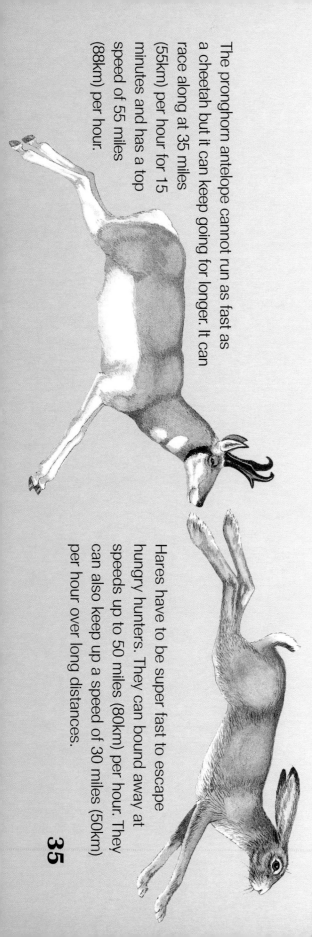

Hares have to be super fast to escape hungry hunters. They can bound away at speeds up to 50 miles (80km) per hour. They can also keep up a speed of 30 miles (50km) per hour over long distances.

Keeping Clean

Staying clean is very important for an animal to keep its fur, feathers, skin, teeth, and claws in top condition. But animals can't just take a bath, comb their hair, or brush their teeth to get clean as you can. Instead, they may use river water or mud to "wash" in. And they use their tongues, fingers, or claws to groom themselves. Some animals get a friend or family member to help them get clean. Some rely on other animals for help. All animals know that being clean is part of being healthy and strong so they look after themselves carefully.

Are flies really dirty?

Houseflies paddle around in dirt and muck and eat and lick up all kinds of disgusting things. But if you watch a fly very carefully you will probably see it rubbing its legs together and brushing its head or wings. Despite its filthy habits, flies are actually very clean insects.

How do cats stay so clean?

All cats are very good at keeping themselves clean. They have very rough tongues, like sandpaper, to lick dirt and pests from their fur. This leopard is having a face wash. It rubs one paw over its face to remove mud, leaves, and insects. Then it licks the paw to make it clean and ready to use again.

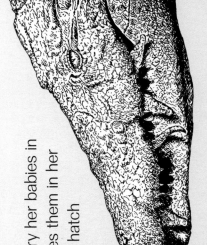

How do animals carry their babies?

Many animals have to carry their babies to keep them safe. A mother orangutan cradles her baby on her stomach as she swings through the forest.

A crocodile cannot carry her babies in her arms. So she carries them in her mouth! When her eggs hatch she gently carries all her babies down to the edge of the water.

36

Do animals take showers?

Elephants love to squirt water over themselves. But this is to help keep them cool in the hot sun, not for washing. They also like to bathe—in mud! The mud helps to rid them of flies and pests that irritate their skin. The mud dries to form an extra "skin" to protect the elephant against sunburn and biting insects.

Which animals help with the cleaning?

Some creatures get other animals to help them keep clean. Like most birds, the jay combs and cleans its feathers with its beak. Sometimes lice and other pests get under the feathers and grab on to the bird's skin. So the jay gets help. It squats in an ants' nest or picks up ants in its beak and puts them in its feathers. The ants nip the lice and pests from the jay's skin.

Do animal parents wash their babies?

Most baby animals cannot wash themselves, so their mother usually does it for them. The mother fox, called a vixen, licks her cubs clean. The fox family lives in a large hole, called a den, until the cubs are several weeks old. The mother keeps the den clean, too. She carries droppings and old bedding outside in her mouth.

Cats, such as this puma, carry their babies in their mouths. The cat holds the kitten by the special loose folds of skin on its neck. The kitten relaxes and it doesn't hurt it one bit!

A kangaroo has a special pouch to carry its baby in. The baby kangaroo, or joey, can travel in its mother's pouch until it is about 10 months old. Then it just gets too big!

Prehistoric Swimmers

Although some dinosaurs could probably swim, none lived in the water all of the time. While dinosaurs ruled the land, other giant reptiles ruled the prehistoric oceans. Mosasaurs, plesiosaurs, and pliosaurs were fierce hunters. They had long jaws full of sharp teeth to snap up fish and other sea creatures. Giant crocodiles and turtles also roamed the ancient seas.

What did prehistoric sea reptiles eat?

Most prehistoric sea reptiles fed on fish, squid, and shellfish called ammonites. Mosasaurs (mo-za-sors) were fast-swimming hunters. They snapped up other sea creatures in their huge mouths, which were filled with rows of sharp teeth. Mosasaurs grew to about 40ft (12m) long. They were the largest ever lizards and are related to today's monitor lizards.

Which were the biggest sea reptiles?

The largest prehistoric sea reptiles were the plesiosaurs (ple-zee-oh-sors) and pliosaurs (ply-oh-sors). Plesiosaurs, like the one shown here, had fat bodies, long necks, and short tails. The biggest grew to longer than a bus. They used their paddle-shaped legs to power them through the water. The pliosaur *Kronosaurus* (kroh-no-saw-rus) was 56ft (17m) long with a head the size of a car!

Are prehistoric reptiles alive today?

Yes, turtles and crocodiles still exist although their prehistoric forms were much bigger. *Deinosuchus* (die-no-sook-us) was a huge 53ft (16m) long crocodile.

Deinosuchus's largest living relative, the saltwater crocodile, is about 23ft (7m) long. It lives along the coasts of Australia and Southeast Asia.

Were ancient ichthyosaurs like dolphins today?

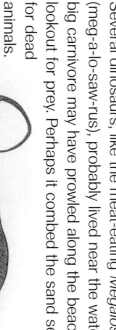

Ichthyosaurs (ik-thee-oh-sors) gave birth to live young, like today's dolphins. The smooth shape of an ichthyosaur was ideal for speeding through water. Its strong tail powered it along and its paddle-like legs were great for steering. Like all sea reptiles, ichthyosaurs had to come to the surface of the sea to breathe.

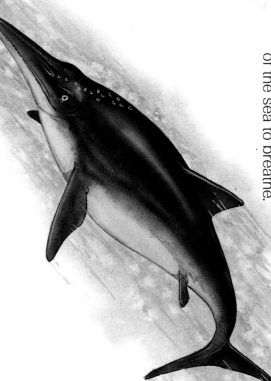

Did dinosaurs live by the sea?

Several dinosaurs, like the meat-eating *Megalosaurus* (meg-a-lo-saw-rus), probably lived near the water. This big carnivore may have prowled along the beach on the lookout for prey. Perhaps it combed the sand searching for dead animals.

Could dinosaurs swim?

No one knows for sure but, like most animals today, dinosaurs could probably swim if they had to. *Cetiosaurus* (see-tee-oh-saw-rus) may have paddled as it searched for food. But it would not have spent much time in the sea. The salt in the water could have damaged its scales and skin.

The prehistoric turtle *Archelon* (ar-kee-lon) was up to 13ft (4m) long, almost twice the size of today's sea turtles.

Archelon's largest living relative, the leatherback turtle, is about 8ft (2.5m) long. The leatherback roams the world's oceans, feeding on jellyfish.

39

Finding Food

Animals can't buy food like people can. They have to hunt and forage for each meal. And each creature has developed its own way of finding its favorite food. Some animals sniff out their food, others have to catch theirs. Some even eat the leftovers that others have left behind. Many creatures carry their meals home or to a place where it is safe to eat—just like a take-out meal!

Which animals like leftovers?

In North America, raccoons sometimes visit houses and search through garbage cans. These animals sniff around everywhere, looking for leftover food. Raccoons will eat almost anything, from bites of burger to chicken bones and fries. Often they grab scraps from take-out meal cartons and hurry away with them—secondhand take-outs!

Who likes nighttime meals?

Baby owls do! A mouse, vole, or lemming is a small snack for a grown-up owl, but it is a full meal for an owl chick. The parent owls are busy all night. They swoop through the dark to grab furry bundles of food, which they carry back to a nestful of hungry owlets.

Do animals cut up their food?

Not all animals cut up their food. In fact, some animals swallow it whole! Many snakes, such as this anaconda, swallow their prey in one, very large mouthful.

Other animals prefer to nibble and gnaw their food. Rodents, like this squirrel, have special teeth to help them nibble and gnaw at foods like nuts and berries.

Do any animals have second helpings?

Rabbits like to eat the same meal twice! They spend many hours nibbling grass and leaves, and taking in goodness from them. They get rid of the leftovers as small, round droppings on the ground. Later, when they feel like a second helping, they eat these droppings to take in any minerals they missed the first time round. When the rabbits produce droppings for the second time, these are much drier and harder.

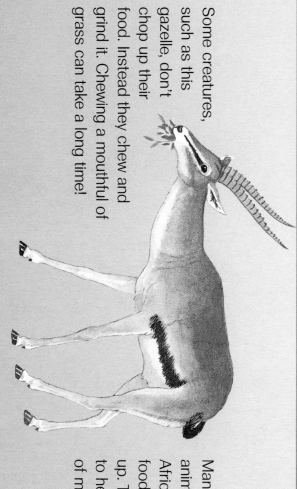

Some creatures, such as this gazelle, don't chop up their food. Instead they chew and grind it. Chewing a mouthful of grass can take a long time!

Many meat-eating animals, like this wild African dog, tear at their food instead of cutting it up. They have sharp teeth to help them break off chunks of meat to swallow.

41

Who enjoys a fish supper?

The favorite take-out of the fisherman bat is fish. Almost every evening, the bat swoops over rivers and lakes, watching for ripples made by fish just below the surface. Then it grabs a victim with its long-clawed feet and flies away to a tree to eat its scaly snack.

Do animals wrap up their food?

Some spiders wrap up their food. The bolas spider does not spin a web. Instead it hangs around on a twig or rock, waiting for unwary insects to wander past. Then it leaps out, lassoes its prey with a silk rope, and ties its meal into a neat bundle. The spider's name comes from the bolas, a rope with weights at the end that South American cowboys use to trip up cattle.

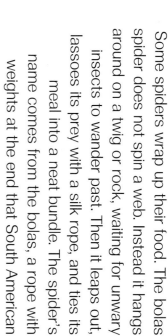

Bugs that Bite

Most creepy crawlies either eat other animals or are themselves eaten. So it is not surprising that they have developed many ways of killing prey and defending themselves. Some, such as bees, wasps, and hornets, have nasty stings in their tails. Others, like spiders and ants, have beastly bites. Some creepy crawlies even have deadly venoms to make up for their tiny size. Many bugs sting or bite if they think they are in danger. Others sting or bite to kill their food or keep it quiet while they eat it!

Can scorpions hurt you?

Yes, if they sting you! Scorpions, like this green scorpion, have a sharp sting at the end of their tails. They use their sting to inject venom into their prey to stop it moving. They also sting other animals if they come too close. Some scorpions' venom is strong enough to kill a person. If you see a scorpion, it's wise to keep away.

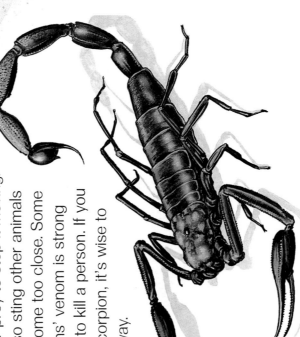

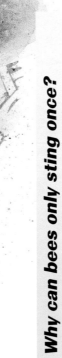

Why can bees only sting once?

A bee's sting is not smooth like a wasp's sting. It has a backward-pointing barb. So, when a bee stings, it can't pull its sting out again. The sting, with its bag of venom, is ripped from the rear end of the bee's body. The bee soon dies. These bumblebees sting to protect their nest from intruders. Their bright yellow and black stripes act as a warning to this mouse which will quickly run away!

Are all bugs poisonous?

No, although some bugs have poisons in their bodies. Many get this poison from their food. Milkweed bugs eat poisonous seed pods. If you ate this food it would make you sick.

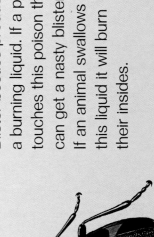

Blister beetles produce a burning liquid. If a person touches this poison they can get a nasty blister. If an animal swallows this liquid it will burn their insides.

42

Do spiders bite?

Spiders have sharp fangs and many can give a venomous bite. Not many spiders have fangs strong enough to cut human skin. But some, like this black widow spider, have venom strong enough to kill you. A spider usually uses its venom to kill its food. It stabs its prey with its fangs and injects the venom. The victim is soon still and quiet. While it is still alive, the victim's insides get dissolved by the juices from the bite.

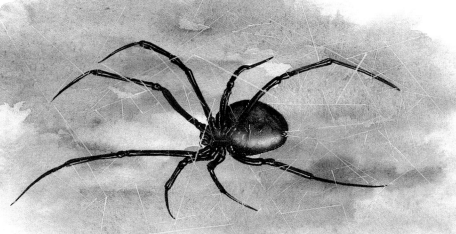

Do some bugs drink blood?

Yes, some bugs, like this mosquito, feed on blood. The mosquito is a kind of fly with a hollow, needlelike mouth. It pushes its sharp mouthparts through your skin, then sucks up your blood. Its saliva (spit) keeps your blood runny while it feeds. This saliva also causes the itchy red lump you get after a mosquito bite.

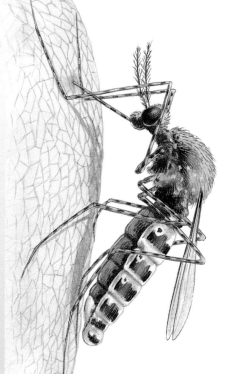

What are stag beetles' giant jaws for?

A stag beetle's jaws may look scary but they're not strong enough to bite you or anything else. Only male beetles have the huge antler-shaped jaws. They are just for show and for fighting other males. Male stag beetles lock jaws and push and shove one another to try to win a battle for a female.

Tiger moths can be deadly dangerous. But, at dawn and dusk, they use a special warning signal. They make a high, squeaky sound to tell hunters that they are not a tasty treat!

Monarch butterflies and caterpillars are poisonous to many other animals. When eaten, the poison makes the hunter's heart beat very fast which makes breathing very difficult.

43

Moving Home

Most of us like to travel to sunny places for our holidays. Animal families travel, too. They like to leave cold places to find somewhere warm for several months each year. The long journeys these animals make are called migrations. Some animals are always on the move. For them every new day brings a new place to live.

Do birds go on very long journeys?

Swallows travel thousands of miles to make sure they are always somewhere warm. In the summer, they live in Europe or North America where they build nests, lay their eggs, and feed their babies on flies, gnats, and other small insects. When the weather starts to get cold, the swallows start another long journey. They fly south from Europe to Africa, or from North America to central and South America, where they can enjoy warm weather for the rest of the year.

How far can insects travel?

As summer ends in Canada and the USA, beautiful monarch butterflies fly south to escape the cold. Some go as far as Mexico, traveling nearly 2000 miles (3000km). When they reach their destination, thousands of the butterflies cluster on cliffs, trees, and cave walls. Here they rest through the warm winter. The next summer they will fly north again.

What do animal babies eat?

Different animals eat different foods—and so do their babies. Mammals, such as this baby panda, all drink their mother's milk. The panda feeds on milk until it is about six months old.

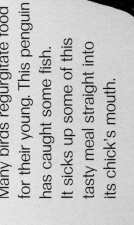

Many birds regurgitate food for their young. This penguin has caught some fish. It sicks up some of this tasty meal straight into its chick's mouth.

Do animals have special winter homes?

In the winter, the female polar bear digs herself a hole in the snow. Here she will give birth to her cubs. The mother and cubs stay in the den through the coldest months. When the cubs are big and strong enough, they leave their cosy den and go out on to the ice. Male polar bears don't have homes. They are always on the move looking for food to eat. They travel across the snow or swim through the icy seas.

Do animals go on winter holidays?

Some animals do. These reindeer live in the cold, open lands of northern Europe during the spring and summer. When fall comes, it is too cold even for them, so they go on a winter holiday. They head south in large herds. As the snow melts in spring the reindeer herds walk north again, munching on the new, juicy plants as they go.

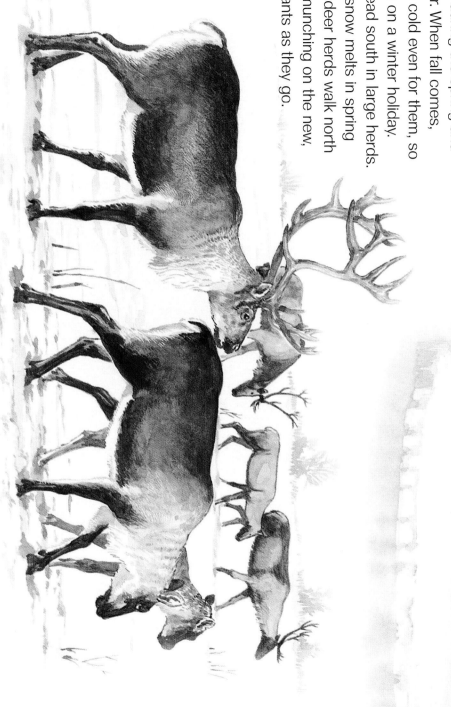

Little tadpoles have to do a lot of growing before they become frogs. Tadpoles feed on algae which they find growing on pondweed.

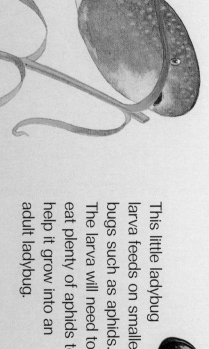

This little ladybug larva feeds on smaller bugs such as aphids. The larva will need to eat plenty of aphids to help it grow into an adult ladybug.

45

Scaly-skinned Dinosaurs

Some pieces of dinosaur skin were hard enough to be preserved and turned to stone. These fossilized remains show that, like living reptiles, some dinosaurs had scaly skins. Scales are made from a tough material called keratin. Scales gave a dinosaur's skin its colors and patterns. They also protected the dinosaur's body. Some dinosaurs had skin covered with bony lumps and bumps for extra protection.

Why did dinosaurs have plates and spines?

Some dinosaurs' bodies were covered with bony plates or spines to protect them. *Stegosaurus* (steg-oh-saw-rus) was the size of a large elephant. This plant-eating dinosaur was protected from attack by huge bony plates along its back. It also had four sharp spines on its tail.

Some experts think its bony plates also helped *Stegosaurus* to control its body temperature, so it did not get too warm or too cold.

Did dinosaurs wear armor?

Some plant-eating dinosaurs were protected by skin like armor. *Saltasaurus* (salt-a-saw-rus) was the first plant-eating giant known to have armor. The skin along its back and sides was packed with pea-size lumps of bone. Its back was also studded with hunks of bone as big as your hand.

Did dinosaurs have feathers?

Not all experts believe dinosaurs had feathers. But most agree that birds have evolved from a group of meat-eating dinosaurs like *Velociraptor* (vel-o-si-rap-tor).

The first known bird was prehistoric *Archaeopteryx* (ar-kee-op-ter-ix). It had a long bony tail, clawed fingers on its hands, and teeth in its beak.

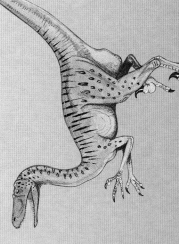

46

Did dinosaurs have different kinds of scales?

Yes, the size and shape of dinosaurs' scales varied. Some scales were joined by bendy skin to allow dinosaurs to move. Body parts that had to bend a lot had smaller scales. *Carnotaurus* (car-noh-taw-rus) was a fierce carnivore. Its fossilized skin showed that it had rows of large, raised, coin-shaped scales along its body. It also had bony horns and rows of big, raised scales on its snout and around its eyes.

What were bone-heads?

"Bone-headed" dinosaurs had thick, bony plates on the tops of their heads. *Stygimoloch* (stij-ee-mol-ok), the "thorny devil", had rows of horns around its bony skull cap. Perhaps, like some wild goats today, *Stygimoloch* head-butted its rivals or enemies. Its bony headgear would have protected its brain from harm.

Why did some dinosaurs have a sail?

No one is sure why some dinosaurs, such as *Spinosaurus* (spy-no-saw-rus), had sails along their backs. *Spinosaurus*'s sail was a flap of skin held up by rods of bone which stuck up from its spine. Maybe it used its sail to attract females or threaten other males. Or perhaps the sail acted as a heating and cooling system. To warm up, the dinosaur turned the flat of its sail toward the sun.

The now extinct diving bird *Hesperornis* (hes-per-or-nis) lived at the end of the Age of Dinosaurs. It looked more like a bird of today, but it still had a bony tail and teeth in its beak.

Birds today, like this pigeon, do not have teeth, clawed wing fingers, or long bony tails. The small tail stumps hold the tail feathers.

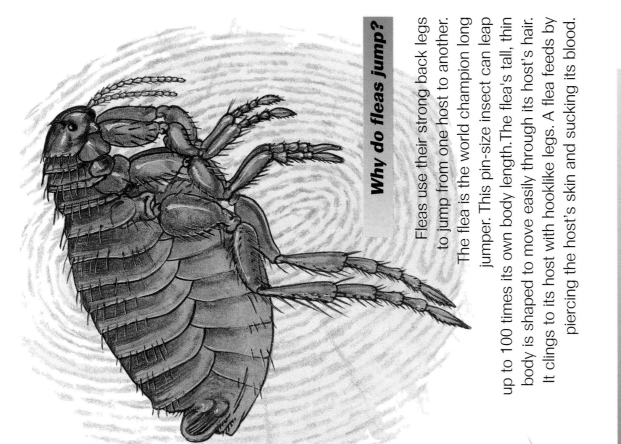

Bloodsuckers!

Minibeasts can live almost anywhere. Some are parasites. They make their homes on, or in, other animals, including humans! A parasite is an animal that gets food and shelter from another animal, called a host. Some parasites live on the host and suck its blood. Others live inside the host's body. Some, such as mites, burrow into the skin. Others live in the blood or gut, where there is a ready supply of food. Many parasites harm their hosts. Some spread diseases that can make people and animals ill or even kill them.

Why do fleas jump?

Fleas use their strong back legs to jump from one host to another. The flea is the world champion long jumper. This pin-size insect can leap up to 100 times its own body length. The flea's tall, thin body is shaped to move easily through its host's hair. It clings to its host with hooklike legs. A flea feeds by piercing the host's skin and sucking its blood.

Can ticks harm you?

Yes, a tick can spread germs when it bites you and sucks your blood. These tiny eight-legged creatures belong to the same group of animals as spiders. The hard tick lives on animals such as sheep and cattle as well as people. It can carry disease from one host to another. The tick clings to the skin of its host by its mouthparts. It can swell to seven times its normal size after a long drink of blood!

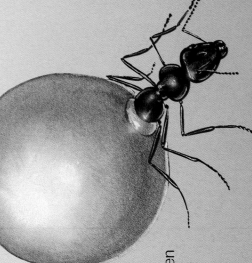

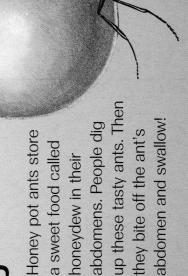

Do people ever eat bugs?

Yes, some bugs are full of goodness, but others are poisonous. Australian Aboriginals like to eat witchetty grubs. These fat white grubs are eaten raw or cooked.

Honey pot ants store a sweet food called honeydew in their abdomens. People dig up these tasty ants. Then they bite off the ant's abdomen and swallow!

Why do some bugs drink blood?

Bugs, such as the benchuca bug from South America, drink blood because it is a good food. This bug stabs a person with its sharp mouthparts and sucks up the blood. Then it flies off to feed on another person. It does not drink enough blood to harm its victims, but it can spread disease. This bug has parasites in its gut that can also make people ill. The parasites are carried into the wound made by the bug as it feeds.

Do bugs really live in beds?

Yes, tiny bed bugs live in furniture, especially beds and carpets. At night they come out to feed on human blood. Bed bugs have long tubelike snouts. They use them to pierce your skin and suck up your blood. Their bites can cause itchy sores.

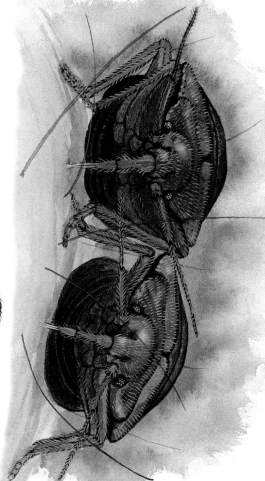

What are nits?

Nits are the eggs of bloodsucking human head lice. An adult louse clings to people's hair with its hook-shaped legs. The lice can crawl from one person's head to another if the heads get close enough to touch. The louse feeds by sucking blood from your scalp. The female louse lays lots of eggs. She glues them to hairs to keep them safe. The eggs hatch in about seven days and the young start to feed.

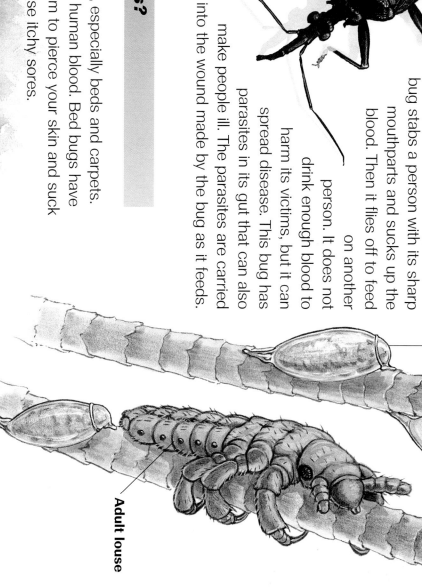

Eggs (nits)

Adult louse

Human hair

Some people like to eat spiders. Edible tarantulas live in the forests of Southeast Asia. Local people kill them and cook them over an open fire to burn off the stinging hairs.

Palolo worms look like green spaghetti. They live in dead coral reefs in the Pacific Ocean. In Samoa and Fiji people catch the worms in nets. They eat them lightly fried or raw!

49

Winter Clothes

Animals don't have woolly clothes to put on when cold weather arrives. They have different ways of dealing with freezing temperatures. Some animals change their natural fur coats as the temperature drops. The thinner hairs of the summer coat fall out, or molt. Longer, thicker hairs grow in their place. The thick winter coat keeps the animal warm and dry. Birds molt, too. They lose their summer feathers and grow thicker plumage to protect them.

Do animals change color in winter?

The thickness of feathers or fur is important in the winter. So is color. Ptarmigans live in the far north, where the winter landscape is white with frost, snow, and ice. So, in winter, the ptarmigan turns white. Its white winter feathers help it to blend in. This helps the ptarmigan hide from hunters. In summer, its brown plumage helps it to hide among the grasses and twigs.

Which cat has the thickest fur coat?

The Siberian tiger is the biggest tiger of all, growing to more than 11ft (3.5m) from nose to tail-tip. And it has the longest and thickest fur of any tiger. Siberia, in northern Asia, is one of the world's coldest places, even in summer. In winter, the Siberian tiger's coat is very pale with thin stripes. This helps it to hide in the snow, as it creeps up on its prey.

What is hibernation?

When winter comes and food supplies are short, some animals go into a deep sleep called hibernation. Like this little dormouse, they will sleep, often for months, until spring arrives.

Legend says groundhogs wake from hibernation on February 2nd, Groundhog Day. It also says that if the animal sees its shadow when it wakes, it sleeps for six more weeks because the clear, cold winter days are not over.

Can body shape keep an animal warm?

Body shape, as well as a thick, furry coat, is important for staying warm in winter. Hares are famous for their long ears. But the snowshoe hare of North America has quite short ears. This is because large body parts that stick out, such as ears and tails, lose a lot of heat. In cold places, animals need to keep in as much body heat as they can.

How do musk oxen keep warm in the snow?

Musk oxen have very thick, very long fur to keep them warm. Each hair is longer than your arm. Musk oxen live in the far north of North America—from Alaska across to Greenland. The countryside is covered with ice and snow for most of the year. The oxen scrape away the snow with their hooves, to uncover plants to eat.

Can animals stay warm in icy seas?

Some animals are specially adapted to stay warm in icy water. The walrus lives in the Arctic seas around the North Pole. It swims in the icy seas and basks on frozen snow. It has hardly any fur, but under its skin, the walrus has a thick layer of body fat, called blubber. This is very good at keeping in body heat. Whales also have thick blubber.

Many bears sleep through the winter, too. But they are not true hibernators. Instead they wake up now and again, when the weather is milder, and go in search of food.

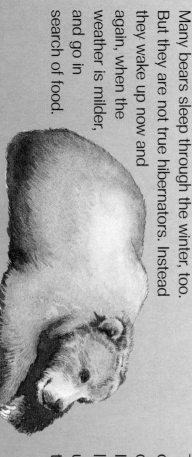

The little brown bat also sleeps out the harsh winter. Bats don't sleep curled up though. Instead, they find somewhere like a snug cave and sleep upside down, hanging by their feet!

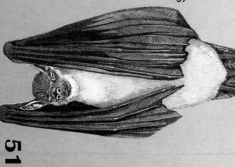

51

Color Codes

Many creepy crawlies are hard to see. The hunters and the hunted both use tricks to help them hide. Some bugs blend in with their background or look like other objects. This is called camouflage. Creepy crawlies are often brightly colored, too. Some use their colors to attract a mate. Other bright bugs match the color of their surroundings. For some minibeasts, bright colors, patterns, and markings act as a warning. They may have stings or venom (poison), or they may taste awful.

Are red bugs dangerous?

People often use the color red as a danger signal and so do other animals. Many bugs, like the red-spotted ladybug, use bright, strong colors to warn other animals that they taste nasty. A hunter may try to eat one, but it soon finds that it makes a horrible-tasting meal. The hunter soon learns not to catch such brightly colored bugs again!

Why are some bugs strange shapes?

Some bugs, like this African devil mantis, are shaped to help them hide among plants. This insect looks like the petals, leaves, and stems of a plant. The mantis is also brightly colored to match the flowers and leaves of the plant that it lives on. It blends in so well that other insects—its prey—do not see it hiding there. This helps the mantis, which is a fierce hunter. As an insect passes by, the mantis grabs it in its spiny front legs.

Do creepy crawlies talk to each other?

Creepy crawlies don't really talk, but they do send signals. The bush cricket sings by rubbing its wings together. Male crickets sing to get a female's attention.

Fireflies need to be able to find each other as they fly through the dark night sky. To do this they flash their lights at one another. Different species have different flash patterns!

Do some bugs pretend to be nasty?

The hoverfly looks like a wasp but it hasn't got a sting. Many animals are fooled by the hoverfly's stripes and keep away. Copying colors and patterns in this way is called mimicry and it can be a means of protection. You can tell a hoverfly from a wasp by the way it flies. A hoverfly darts about and hovers in the air like a mini-helicopter.

Why are wasps black and yellow?

The bold yellow and black stripes of this common wasp are easy to see. They give other animals a clear warning: "Stay away! Or I'll sting you!" Other creatures know that these colors mean danger. So they keep out of the wasp's way. That's what you should do, too. Leave wasps and bees alone and they will soon buzz off back to their nests.

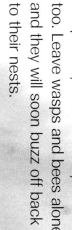

Are all butterflies brightly colored?

No, some butterflies are white or pale colored. But many butterflies do use bright colors to attract a mate. This blue morpho butterfly lives in tropical forests where there is little light. When they are ready to mate, groups of blue morphos gather in forest clearings. Their brilliant colors glow as they flit and dance in shafts of bright sunlight.

Some bugs use vibration signals to talk to each other. A male field spider visiting a female can tug a thread of her web to tell her he's there. She can send a message back by tugging her end!

Bugs may need to give each other messages when they are near one another, too. One way an ant can talk to another ant is by tapping the other ant with its antennae.

53

Plant-eating Dinosaurs

Most dinosaurs had a tasty meal within easy reach—plants. We call plant-eating animals herbivores. Herbivorous dinosaurs came in all shapes and sizes, and they fed on all kinds of plants. The shape of a dinosaur's teeth and jaws are clues to what plants it ate. Some dinosaur fossils even have the remains of their last meal in their stomachs. Conifers were the most common trees at the time of the dinosaurs. Conifer needles are tough and do not contain a lot of goodness. So many herbivores had to spend nearly all day eating.

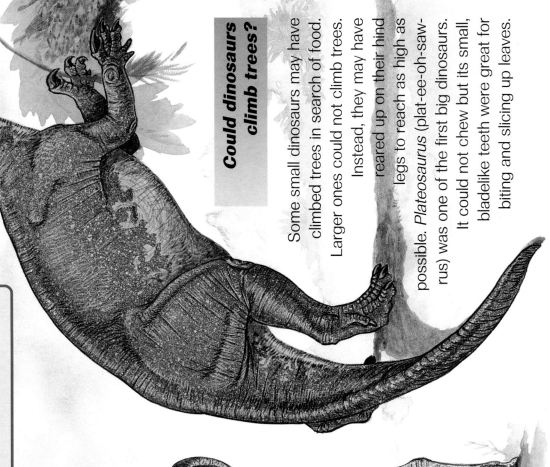

Could dinosaurs climb trees?

Some small dinosaurs may have climbed trees in search of food. Larger ones could not climb trees. Instead, they may have reared up on their hind legs to reach as high as possible. *Plateosaurus* (plat-ee-oh-saw-rus) was one of the first big dinosaurs. It could not chew but its small, bladelike teeth were great for biting and slicing up leaves.

Did all dinosaurs have teeth?

No, some dinosaurs, such as *Gallimimus* (gal-ih-my-mus), had beaklike mouths with no teeth. *Gallimimus* looked like a large ostrich and could outrun most predators. It ate mostly leaves and fruit but may have pecked up tasty insects and small lizards, too.

Were all dinosaur teeth the same?

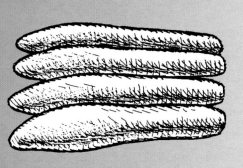

Dinosaur teeth came in all different shapes and sizes. *Iguanodon* (ig-wa-no-don) had several rows of sharp leaf-shaped teeth, which were perfect for chewing and chopping plants.

Diplodocus (dip-lo-doh-cus) could not chew. Instead, this dinosaur's teeth were peg-shaped to help it strip the leaves from branches of trees. It then swallowed the leaves whole.

Which dinosaurs had the most teeth?

Duck-billed dinosaurs, such as *Kritosaurus* (cry-toh-saw-rus), had hundreds of teeth. These teeth were broad and flat with sharp edges and ridges—great for grinding up plants. *Kritosaurus* could probably chew up almost anything, even hard roots and woody stems.

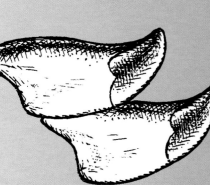

Triceratops (try-serra-tops) had hundreds of sharp teeth. When it closed its mouth, the upper and lower teeth moved like garden shears, slicing its plant food into tiny pieces.

Meat-eating dinosaurs had very different teeth from plant-eaters. *Megalosaurus*'s (meg-a-lo-saw-rus) huge, pointed, razor-sharp teeth curved backward to help it hold onto prey.

Why did dinosaurs swallow stones?

Many plant-eating dinosaurs, such as *Mamenchisaurus* (ma-men-chee-saw-rus), could not chew. This dinosaur raked the leaves off trees with its strong, small teeth, and swallowed them whole. So, like many dinosaurs, *Mamenchisaurus* swallowed stones to help break up the food in its gut. The stones acted like a grinding mill. They moved around in its stomach, mashing up its leafy meal into a pulp.

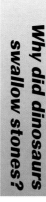

Out After Dark

Most people are active during the day and sleep at night. Animals that behave like this are called diurnal. Some animals are active at night. They are called nocturnal animals. These animals need to have special equipment to help them find their way around in the dark without bumping into things. Animals that are nocturnal often have huge eyes to help them see in very dim light. Some use large whiskers to feel for objects they might not be able to see. Nocturnal animals also need keen noses to sniff out food and they have sensitive ears to listen out for danger.

Who doesn't get home before dark?

Most animals like to be safe at home by the time the sun sets but these little blue penguins do not finish fishing and feeding in the sea until after dark. Then they waddle quickly across the beach to the safety of their burrows in the dunes. They live in tunnels along the seashores of southern Australia.

Do animals cry in the dark?

The bushbaby is an animal that lives in the African forests. It got its name because of the cry it makes at night. It sounds like the screaming wail of a human baby. This hand-sized relative of monkeys also looks babyish because it has a snub nose and huge eyes to help it to see in the dark. But a crying bushbaby is not in pain. It cries to warn other bushbabies to keep out of the small area, or territory, where it lives and feeds.

Can animals glow in the dark?

Yes, some animals do actually glow in the dark. The firefly squid produces a blue-white light. It can change the color and brightness of its light. This helps it to blend in with its watery surroundings.

Some starfish produce a glowing light. This starfish lives over half a mile (1km) below the sea's surface. Its glow warns hunters such as fish or crabs that it doesn't taste very nice!

56

Do birds sing at night?

Most birds sleep after dark but some nocturnal birds sing and hunt at night. The nightjar sings its jarring, churring song—it sounds like a small motorcycle engine after dark. And it flies at night—swooping over fields and between trees as it catches its food of flying insects. It has good eyesight and a wide beak to help it hunt. By day, the nightjar sits quite still on the ground or in a tree, looking like dead leaves or a branch.

Can animals hunt without daylight?

Most cats, such as this black panther, are adapted to hunt unseen at night. On a dark night, few creatures would see the black panther creeping silently towards them. But this big cat has good eyesight, and can see them! A black panther is really a very dark-colored type of leopard. Daylight reveals its black spots against the slightly paler fur. Black leopards are common in parts of Southeast Asia.

Can noises help animals "see" in the dark?

Bats, such as the horseshoe bat, find their way around in the dark using squeaking noises. The bat makes very high squeaks, clicks and other sounds. The echoes of these sounds bounce off nearby objects, such as trees and walls or moths and mosquitoes. The bat listens to the pattern of these echoes. It can then find its way or can catch food, even in total darkness.

The deep-sea angler fish lives in darkness. Above its mouth, this fish has a special fin with a light at the end of it. This lures little fish for the angler to eat!

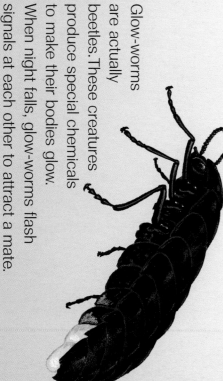

Glow-worms are actually beetles. These creatures produce special chemicals to make their bodies glow. When night falls, glow-worms flash signals at each other to attract a mate.

57

Animal Gifts

Animals have many different ways of making friends. Lots of creatures give each other presents, especially to their mates when they are courting. An adult sometimes gives its partner a surprise present at other times of the year, just to make sure he or she doesn't forget they are mates. Many animal parents look after their babies very carefully, feeding and protecting them. Some animal parents even give their babies "toys" to play with!

What "toys" do baby animals enjoy?

This right whale baby is enormous, almost as big as a car, so it needs large toys too. Its mother looks after it well and protects it from hungry enemies, such as sharks and killer whales. The mother may give her baby a present of a tree trunk that has floated out to sea. The baby whale has great fun bashing the "toy" about in the water with its flippers and tail.

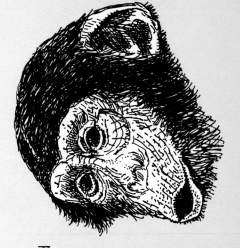

How do chimpanzees talk to each other?

Some animals talk to each other. But not in the same way that people do. Chimpanzees make faces to tell each other how they feel. This chimp is resting.

This chimp is telling the others that he has found food. He also makes special hooting noises, called pant-hoots, just to make sure they understand!

58

Can a gift save an animal's life?

It can certainly save this male wolf spider's life! For a gift, he catches a fly or other insect and ties it with his silk thread. Then he gives the neatly wrapped parcel to the female. While she undoes the present and eats it, he quickly mates with her. The male spider is smaller than the female and, at mating time, she may eat him. So it is important for the male not to forget this present!

Do animals give each other food?

Some birds offer food to their partners. These gifts help the male and female to stay friends. The male kingfisher gives his mate a fish. He offers it head-first, so that she can swallow it without choking. These tasty presents help to keep the partners together.

Which animals give grooming gifts?

Many apes and monkeys groom each other. These gibbons are long-armed apes that swing through the trees of Southeast Asia. They comb and scratch through each other's fur and pick out dirt, leaves, and pests. They may offer the pests, such as lice and fleas, to each other to eat as tasty titbits!

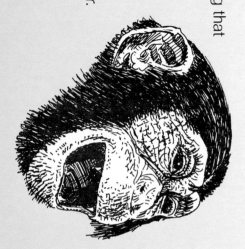

This chimp is showing that he is angry. His eyes and mouth are open and his long, sharp teeth are bared. This is a show of aggression and anger.

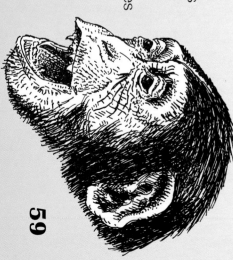

This chimp looks like he is laughing! His mouth is open and his lips are relaxed. The chimp is telling other chimpanzees that he is in a playful mood.

Bug-eyed!

Minibeasts come in many shapes and varieties and so do their eyes. Some creepy crawlies have simple eyes that can only tell light from dark. Spiders have two, four, six, or eight eyes to spot their prey very quickly. Other bugs have no eyes at all. They live underground, or in caves or deep water, where there is little or no light. Without light, you cannot see, so eyes are useless. Most insects are "bug-eyed". They see the world as a jigsaw of tiny pictures. This is because an insect's eyes are made up of lots of little lenses. Each lens produces a tiny part of the overall picture.

Can spiders see well?

Yes, most spiders can. Simple eyes around the head help them spot their prey very quickly. The zebra jumping spider has eight simple eyes of various sizes. Three pairs of eyes on the sides of its head help the spider spot an animal moving nearby. Then it stalks its prey using its main, central eyes, which give a clearer view. It judges how far away its meal is, then jumps for the kill!

Where are a snail's eyes?

Snails, like this giant African land snail, have eyes on the tips of their tentacles. Eyes on stalks can be very useful. The snail can extend its tentacles to have a good look around, then pull them back into its head for safety. A snail's eyes cannot see any details, only blurred patches of light and dark. But that's enough for this giant snail—the biggest in the world—to find its food. It gobbles up crops, dead animals, and even other snails.

Do insects have noses to smell with?

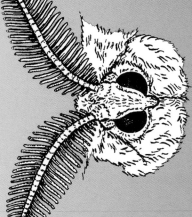

Insects can smell, but they do not have noses. They pick up smells with their feelers, or antennae. Ants use feelers to sniff out food, find their nest, and to tell friends from enemies.

Many male moths have large feathery feelers to pick up smells. Male emperor moths can smell females up to 7 miles (11km) away!

60

Which insect has the biggest eyes?

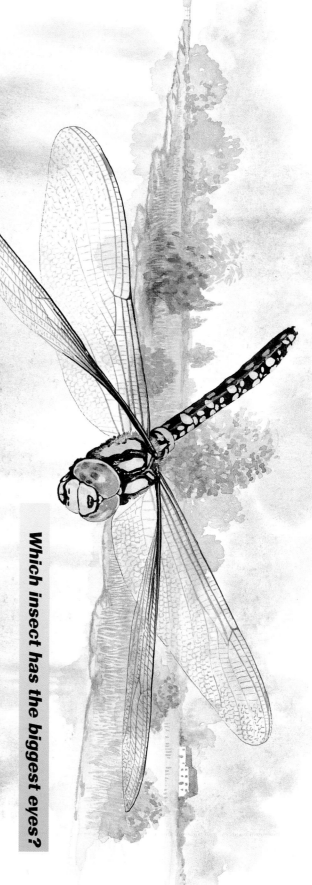

The biggest eyes in the insect world belong to the dragonfly. Its eyes are enormous compared with the size of its body. On the same scale, a human's eyes would be over 3ft (1m) across! An emperor dragonfly's eyes can have up to 30,000 lenses. Each lens faces a slightly different way, giving the insect an all-around view. This fierce hunter can spot its prey up to 3ft (1m) away.

Proper eyes would not be much use beneath the ground, so an earthworm doesn't have any. However, patches of skin on the upper part of its head can tell light from dark. These warn the earthworm when it is near to the surface. This giant Australian earthworm is a real monster. It grows up to 12ft (3.5m) long and squirts a foul-smelling liquid at its enemies!

Which bug can see in air and under water?

Have you ever tried seeing under water? If you have, you will know that things look blurred. This is because our eyes are made to see in air. The whirligig beetle spends its life swimming round and round on the surface of a pond. It can see in both air and water. How does it do it? Simple! Its eyes are divided into two parts. The top halves look into the air above the surface of the pond. The bottom halves look down into the water.

Butterflies have antennae shaped like tiny clubs. They use them to sniff out food plants. But they don't use their antennae for tasting. They check whether food tastes good with their feet!

The long-horned beetle gets its name from its extra-long antennae. The male beetle's antennae help him sniff out a mate from several miles away.

61

Prehistoric Signals

Dinosaurs could not talk to one another in the way we do, so they communicated in other ways. They probably used sounds, smells, touch, and visual signals, just as animals do today. Herds of animals often flash signals to each other. A sudden flash of color can be a warning of danger. Dinosaurs probably used lots of signals to give different messages to each other. The signals could say, "Keep away! I'm dangerous". Or "Run! An enemy is nearby!" Or "I'm big and strong. Would you like to mate with me?"

Like reptiles today, most dinosaurs could probably hiss or grunt. Large ones may have roared. Some, such as hadrosaurs, probably made lots of different sounds. Many hadrosaurs had strange bony crests or horns on their heads. The hadrosaur called *Parasaurolophus* (parra-saw-ro-lo-fus) had a hollow bony pipe on top of its head. The pipe was connected to air tubes in its nose and throat. Experts think it could make sounds as it breathed in and out. Perhaps it kept in touch with its herd by trumpeting to them.

Could dinosaurs change color?

Some living reptiles, such as chameleons, can change the color of their skin. No one knows if dinosaurs could do the same or what color their skin was. Some horn-faced dinosaurs, such as *Chasmosaurus* (kaz-mo-saw-rus), had a large neck frill. Perhaps this frill was brightly colored. The dinosaur may have shaken its head to send messages to other *Chasmosaurus* or to scare away enemies.

Did dinosaurs have tongues?

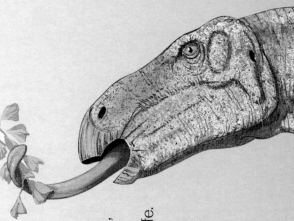

There are no fossils of tongues, but experts know dinosaurs had tongues from fossil bones. Perhaps, like lizards today, *Struthiomimus* (stroo-thee-oh-my-mus) smelled the air with its tongue.

Maybe plant-eaters, like *Iguanodon* (ig-wa-no-don), had long, muscular tongues, like today's giraffe. These would have been great for pulling shoots and leaves from plants.

62

Could dinosaurs communicate with their noses?

Most dinosaurs had well-developed nostrils. A good sense of smell would have helped them to find their food and smell friends or enemies. *Edmontosaurus* (ed-mont-oh-saw-rus) may have used a large flap of skin on top of its nose to make a noise. Perhaps it blew this up like a balloon to give a sound and make a color signal.

Did dinosaurs display like birds?

Many dinosaurs had head crests, spines or neck ruffs. Perhaps these were displayed to attract females or warn rivals. *Psittacosaurus* (si-tak-oh-saw-rus) had a beaklike mouth, just like a puffin. Perhaps its beak was brightly colored and other dinosaurs in its group could recognize it by its striped nose.

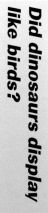

Did dinosaurs fight?

Yes, some dinosaurs sent messages by fighting. *Pachycephalosaurus* (pak-ee-sef-a-lo-saw-rus) had a thick bony skull. Its dome-shaped head looked like a crash helmet. Perhaps male *Pachycephalosaurus* had noisy head-butting contests, like today's goats. The winner may have become leader of the herd. Or perhaps they fought over female dinosaurs.

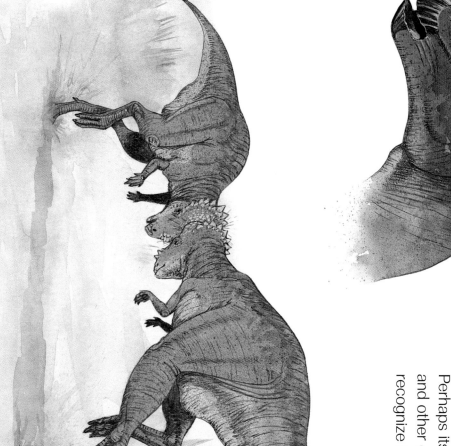

Could dinosaurs communicate with their noses?

Meat-eating dinosaurs, like *Ceratosaurus* (serra-toh-saw-rus), may have had rough tongues like cats today. The rough surface would have helped scrape the last scraps of meat from bones.

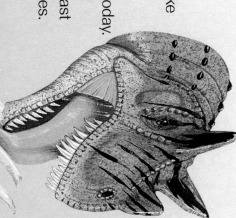

Penguins need to catch slippery fish. They have small spines on their tongues to help them do this. Perhaps fish-eaters, like *Baryonyx* (bar-ee-on-ix), had spiny tongues to help them, too.

63

Babies All Alone

In the animal world, it is common for young animals to be left alone. They stay in their nest or burrow while their parents go out to feed. These babies are usually well hidden and know by instinct that they must keep quiet to stay safe from their enemies. Even if their parents are away for half a day or more, the babies don't make a fuss. They know that their lives depend on staying hidden.

Are all baby animals left alone?

Some animals only leave their babies alone when there is danger about. Usually, a young kangaroo lives in its mother's pouch, which is a pocket of skin on her front. The baby only comes out to play or feed. But if there is an enemy near, the mother may leave her baby hiding in a bush so that she can run faster and lead the enemy away. She returns later to collect her baby.

Do animals ever shut their babies in?

Sometimes, when animals leave their babies alone, they shut them in to keep them safe. The platypus lives in rivers and lakes in eastern Australia. It has webbed feet, a furry body, and a mouth like a duck's bill. Baby platypuses live in a long tunnel in the river bank. When she goes out to eat, the mother blocks the burrow entrance with mud. The babies are alone but safe.

When does a baby animal leave home?

Baby hippos stay close to their mothers for the first few years of their lives. Sometimes a young female hippo will stay in the same herd as its mother for all her life.

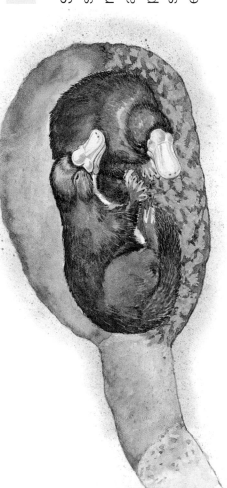

Macaws stay with their parents for up to two years. The young macaw will leave the nest when the parents have more babies.

How long can a baby animal be left?

A baby albatross may be left all alone on a cold, windy island for two or three weeks! The albatross is a huge, white sea bird with very long wings. The baby albatross is a large ball of fluffy feathers. Its parents fly over the sea catching fish. When the adults do return they bring back smelly, half-digested fish for their baby to eat.

Why do baby penguins huddle together?

Baby penguins are born in the coldest place on Earth, the ice-covered land of Antarctica. Even a freezer is warmer! The parent penguins waddle off and dive into the ocean to catch fish and other sea animals. The babies are left alone and stay in a group, huddled together against the cold. They don't need to worry about enemies. It is too cold for any other animals to live there.

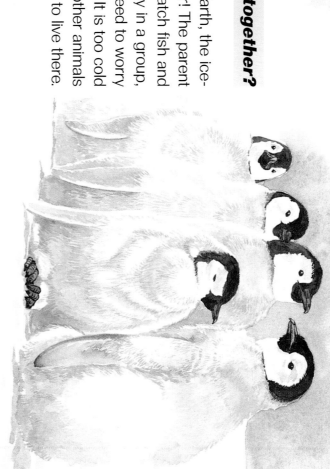

How do animal babies stay hidden?

Sometimes animal babies have special camouflage to help them stay hidden. A young deer is called a fawn. Unlike its parents, the fawn has white spots on its fur. As it lies in the grass under a bush, the fawn's pattern merges with the shadows and patches of sunlight. This makes it hard for enemies to spot the fawn.

An elephant seal mother won't leave her pup's side for a month. While she feeds her baby, she never eats at all. After a month, she swims away and the baby has to take care of itself.

Green turtle babies never see their mother. Her eggs hatch two to three months after she left them buried on the beach. The babies look after themselves.

65

Doing the Housework

Animals know they need to keep their nests and burrows clean and tidy. If they didn't, their homes would soon be deep in skin, feathers, or fur—not to mention fleas and piles of droppings! Many animals spend a lot of time tidying their homes and removing rubbish. Some animals even have a big clear out several times a day! They don't have vacuum cleaners or brushes. Instead they use their feet, claws, and mouths to clear away bits of rubbish and uneaten food.

Do animals like to have clean beds?

Badgers do! These animals are known to be very clean. Every few days, they clear out their underground home of tunnels and rooms, called a set. The badgers pull out all the old leaves, grass, and moss, which they use for bedding. Then they collect clean, dry bedding and take it into the set.

Do animal parents clean up after their babies?

Harvest mice live in a nest the size and shape of a tennis ball. It is made out of woven grass stems. The mother harvest mouse is always going in and out through the small entrance hole, carrying rubbish in her mouth. She is clearing out droppings and bits of leftover food that her babies have not eaten.

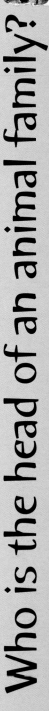

Who is the head of an animal family?

Many groups of animals have one leader who decides where and when to hunt and feed. Others, like this pair of swans, work as a partnership. They look after each other and their family together.

Wolves often live in large groups called packs. There may be more than one wolf family in a pack. So there is always a pack leader. The leader is the strongest male wolf. The pack follows him on its hunting trips.

How often do animals tidy up?

Blue tit parents give their nest a good clean several times each day. A blue tit nest may be occupied by more than ten chicks who sometimes leave bits of their caterpillar dinners. So, like many birds, blue tits use their beaks to flick bits of old food and droppings from their nests.

Do animals have cleaners?

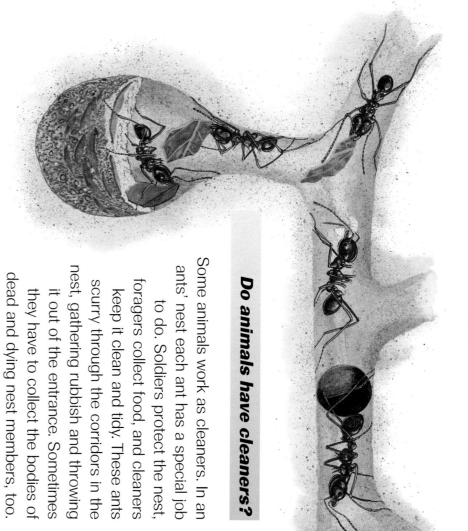

Some animals work as cleaners. In an ants' nest each ant has a special job to do. Soldiers protect the nest, foragers collect food, and cleaners keep it clean and tidy. These ants scurry through the corridors in the nest, gathering rubbish and throwing it out of the entrance. Sometimes they have to collect the bodies of dead and dying nest members, too.

Do animals like to be comfortable?

Cats certainly do. All cats, big and small, are neat and clean. They would never lie down to sleep on lumpy stones or sharp twigs. They remove any pieces of rubbish from their favorite resting place before settling down for a catnap.

Gorillas live in small groups made up of one male leader, one or two other males, and several females and young. Old males are called silverbacks because they have silvery hair on their backs.

Some animal families have female leaders. An elephant herd is led by a female. This elephant, called the matriarch, is old and wise.

Dinosaur Hunters

Many dinosaurs were carnivores. They hunted, killed, and ate other animals. Like carnivores today, meat-eating dinosaurs caught their prey in different ways. Some were fierce hunters, chasing after their victims. Others hid in the undergrowth, waiting to leap out on their prey. Some dinosaurs hunted alone. Others formed savage packs. Some meat-eating dinosaurs were scavengers, feeding on dead or dying animals.

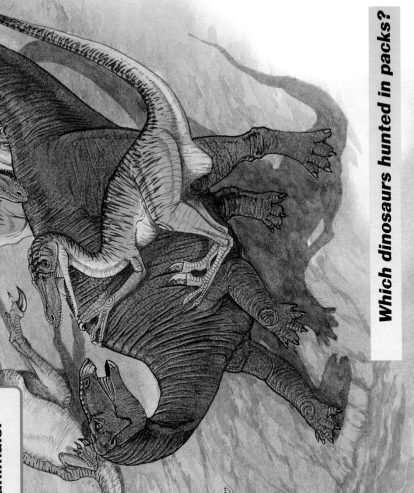

Which dinosaurs hunted in packs?

Some of the smaller dinosaurs, such as *Velociraptor* (vel-o-si-rap-tor), may have hunted in packs. This would have helped them to attack much larger animals. *Velociraptor* had sharp teeth and huge claws for tearing and slashing flesh. Even a large dinosaur could have been killed by a pack of these fierce predators.

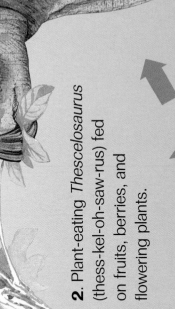

What is a food chain?

A food chain is a list of which animals eat what. 70 million years ago it may have been like this:

1. Plants, at the start of the food chain, make their food using sunlight.

2. Plant-eating *Thescelosaurus* (thess-kel-oh-saw-rus) fed on fruits, berries, and flowering plants.

68

Which were the biggest meat-eaters?

The biggest meat-eating dinosaurs were the carnosaurs. They all walked on their strong hind legs and had huge heads and tiny arms. At 40ft (12m) long, *Tarbosaurus* (tar-bo-saw-rus) was one of the largest. Each razor-sharp tooth was bigger than your hand. *Tarbosaurus* could move fast and may have sprinted after its prey.

3. *Dromaeosaurus* (dro-mee-oh-saw-rus) was a fast-moving carnivore. It fed on plant-eaters such as *Thescelosaurus*.

4. *Tyrannosaurus rex* (ty-ran-oh-saw-rus reks) was at the top of the chain. This fierce hunter preyed on plant-eaters and other meat-eaters.

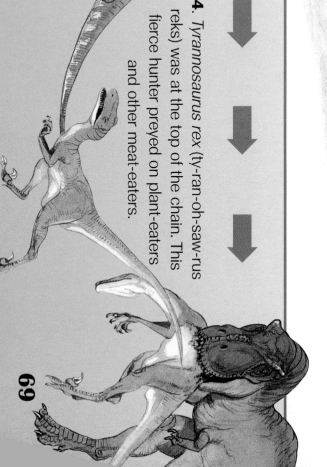

69

Were dinosaur hunters fast runners?

Many meat-eating dinosaurs were very fast movers. *Dilophosaurus* (dy-lo-fo-saw-rus) may have been able to run twice as fast as you! This long-legged hunter was armed with thin, daggerlike teeth. These were great for jabbing and killing small prey and for tearing off lumps of meat.

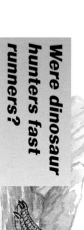

Did dinosaurs eat fish?

Many dinosaurs lived near water, so it is possible that some ate fish. Experts think *Baryonyx* (bar-ee-on-ix) fished for its supper. Maybe it waded through the water, hooking out fish with its big claws like bears do today. *Baryonyx*'s long, narrow jaws were full of small sharp teeth. Perhaps, like a crocodile, it used them to hold slippery fish before swallowing them whole.

Woodland Homes

More animals make their homes in forests and woods than anywhere else on Earth. The trees provide all sorts of different foods, including leaves, shoots, fruits, and roots. They also provide a place to shelter and to raise a family. Thousands of different kinds of animals build homes and nests among the trees.

Which bird is a noisy neighbor?

The green woodpecker can make a lot of noise! This bird "drums" on a tree with a series of very fast pecks, making a noise like a machine gun. The woodpecker makes tiny holes with its long, sharp beak. It searches under the bark for beetles, grubs, and other small animals. Its skull and neck are very strong, so it doesn't get a headache!

Do bear families live in the woods?

Brown bears live in forests and mountain areas in northwest North America, where they are sometimes called grizzlies. They also live in parts of Europe and across northern Asia. Brown bears eat almost any food, from leaves and fruits to insects, fish, and young deer. But beware of bears, especially a mother with her cub. To protect her baby she will charge and fight anyone who comes near.

What is a territory?

A territory is the area an animal lives in. A male lion defends his territory and his family, or pride, from other lion prides. He roars loudly to scare enemies and other lions away.

Pet male Siamese fighting fish are so aggressive that two cannot be kept in the same tank. In the wild, one swims away to find a new home.

Do animals warn each other of danger?

Some animals do. Deer, such as the white-tailed deer, are well adapted to life in open woodland, where they graze on shoots and leaves. When in danger, they can hide in the thick undergrowth, or race to safety among the tree trunks. When the deer runs, the bright flash of white fur beneath its tail acts as a warning to other members of the herd.

What is there to eat in the forests?

There are lots of different foods to find in forests and woods. The hedgehog searches for slugs, snails, worms, grubs, and other small snacks. This prickly animal is a relative of moles and shrews. The average hedgehog has about 5,000 sharp spines. It rolls up into a ball to protect itself from predators.

What is dangerous in the woods?

Many predators hunt in the forests. The gray wolf was once common in woods across North America, Europe, and Asia. But many woods have been cut down and the wolves have had to find new homes. People also hunt wolves because they attack farm animals.

You can hear a howler monkey from several miles away. Its noisy scream tells other howler monkeys exactly which bit of the forest it lives in.

You may have a little blue tit, or even a blue tit family, living in your garden. Your garden is their territory. They'll make sure no other blue tits move into their patch!

Moms and Dads

Animal parents lead very busy lives. Whether they are part of a large group of animals or whether they live alone, they have to work hard to feed their babies and keep them safe. They also have to look after themselves. Animal parents often have to leave their young for a while, to hunt for food or chase away enemies. When this happens, they have to find ways to make sure their babies are not going to get into trouble.

Do animals have babysitters?

When animals go off to find food, they may have to leave their young behind. While parent giraffes are feeding, they leave their babies with other baby giraffes in a group called a crèche. Sometimes "aunties" babysit for the young giraffes and keep them safe.

How many babies do animals have?

The little harvest mouse works hard to look after her babies. She has up to 12 babies at once and can have up to seven litters of young in a single year!

Some animals, such as the giant anteater, have only one baby at a time. The mother anteater takes extra special care of her baby, carrying it on her back.

72

Do some animals live in a commune?

In a large group of 30 meerkats there will be several families. The adults take it in turns to look after one another's young so the other parents can look for food or defend the burrows against enemies. Meerkats live in long, winding burrows in the grasslands of Africa. They eat all kinds of food, from insects, lizards, birds, and other small creatures to leaves, seeds, and fruits.

Do animals adopt other babies?

Some animals adopt other animals' babies but they don't always know they are doing it. This tiny robin is feeding a big baby cuckoo. The mother cuckoo lays her egg in another bird's nest then flies away. When the baby cuckoo hatches, it pushes the other bird's eggs out of the nest. The robin thinks the cuckoo chick is hers so she and her mate look after it.

Do animals know who their parents are?

Some animals mistake a different animal for their mother. When baby birds hatch, the first thing they usually see is their real mother so they follow her. But sometimes eggs get mixed up. A hen may sit on a duck's eggs by mistake. When the ducklings hatch, they see the hen and think she is their mother!

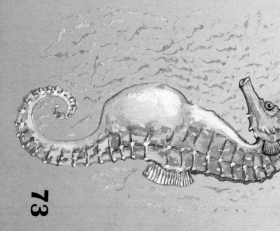

The male seahorse is the one who takes care of the eggs and he is the father of one of the largest animal families of all. Up to 1,000 little seahorse babies can hatch in one family!

Some animals have lots and lots of babies. The fer-de-lance snake gives birth to around 80 wriggling little snakes. But the snake doesn't look after her babies. Only a few will survive.

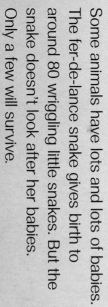

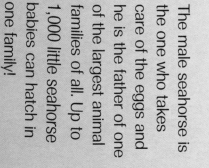

73

Bug Pests

Some people are afraid of creepy crawlies, especially spiders. Often there is no good reason as the creatures are harmless. With other minibeasts, it is wise to be careful. Some bugs are pests, causing harm or damage to crops and plants. Others can make farm animals and pets ill. Some bugs spread germs or diseases in humans. Others may bite, sting, or poison you. Minibeasts can burrow into wood and destroy your homes. They may even eat your clothes!

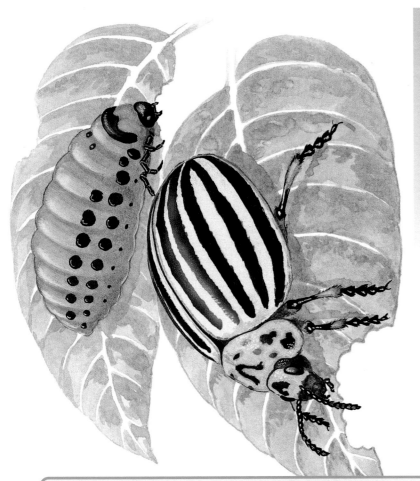

Do bugs eat our food?

Yes, many bugs eat the same plants that we do. Some, such as Colorado beetles, can cause a lot of damage. The black-and-yellow adults feed on potato leaves. So do their orange-red larvae. They can destroy huge fields of potatoes in a few days. If farmers see this beetle they use special sprays to kill them.

Why don't people like spiders?

Not everyone hates spiders. Some people like them and keep them as pets. People often find big hairy spiders, like tarantulas, scary. But many of them are harmless. Some can give you a nasty bite, but they hardly ever kill people. Often small spiders are far more dangerous. Australian redbacks and North American black widow spiders are much more deadly.

Are some bugs our friends?

Yes, some creepy crawlies are useful little helpers. The wolf spider helps people by hunting and eating caterpillars that can do serious damage to crops.

People may be scared of being stung by bees but this event is rare and bees do provide us with a sweet treat – honey! They also give us beeswax, which is used to make polish.

74

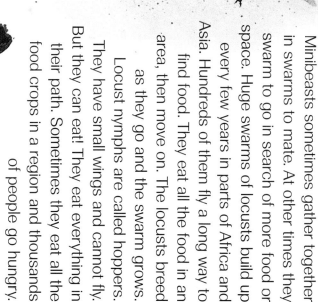

Why do bugs swarm?

Minibeasts sometimes gather together in swarms to mate. At other times they swarm to go in search of more food or space. Huge swarms of locusts build up every few years in parts of Africa and Asia. Hundreds of them fly a long way to find food. They eat all the food in an area, then move on. The locusts breed as they go and the swarm grows.

Locust nymphs are called hoppers. They have small wings and cannot fly. But they can eat! They eat everything in their path. Sometimes they eat all the food crops in a region and thousands of people go hungry.

Can harmless bugs still make you ill?

Yes, some harmless bugs can hurt you by spreading diseases. In Africa, a disease called sleeping sickness, or nagana, is spread by the tsetse fly. The fly bites an animal or person that has the disease. As the fly sucks their blood, it takes in the germs. Then the tsetse fly flies off to its next victim. The fly "injects" the animal or person with the harmful germs as it bites them.

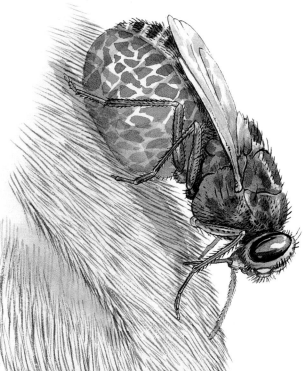

Do bugs eat clothes?

Yes, the caterpillars of clothes moths will make a meal of your gloves—or any other clothes they can find! The caterpillars change into pupae and then into adult moths. The adults lay their eggs on your clothes. The eggs hatch into caterpillars—and so the cycle starts again.

The silk moth is a very special bug. The caterpillar of this moth spins a fine silken thread to make its cocoon. People collect this thread to make silk fabric.

Snails are a nuisance to gardeners—they like to eat plants. Luckily for us, ground beetles like to eat snails!

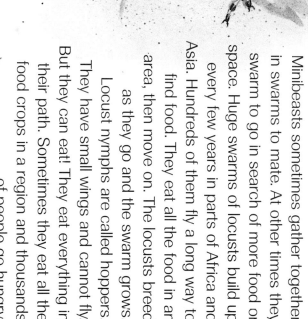

Song and Dance

Animals do sing and dance, but not just for fun. In the spring, adult animals begin their courtship. This means they try to attract a mate, often by putting on song-and-dance displays. The males are usually the ones to sing and dance. Sometimes their skin, fur, or feathers change color, too. Their calls and movements may seem strange to us. But to the female animals these performances are just too good to miss!

Which creatures sing in the pond?

In spring, the chorus of male frogs fills the evening air. "Ree-deep, ree-deep." "Rivet-rivet." "Wurp-wurp." The males gather in ponds and swamps to croak and croon love songs to the females. Each type of frog has a different call. Soon the females arrive to choose the best male of their type as a mate.

Which bird is a star performer?

One of nature's most spectacular sights is the courtship display of male birds of paradise. These birds live in the tropical forests of Southeast Asia. They sing loudly, shake their brilliant feathers, hop about, and sometimes even hang upside down from branches. The dull brown females watch the splendid performance.

Which animals make the most noise?

Bugs can make a lot of noise, too. Male crickets rub their wings together to make their loud song. The male cricket sings to attract females, and to tell other male crickets to stay away!

Some animals make barely any sound. Others like to be heard! Howler monkeys are some of the loudest mammals. These monkeys can be heard from 5 miles (8km) away!

76

Are all animal songs tuneful?

No, the noise a male koala makes is a deep, bellowing, growling sound. Koalas live in the gum trees of eastern Australia. The noise the koala makes echoes through the night air. He is telling other male koalas to keep away from his patch of forest, otherwise he'll fight them. He is also asking female koalas if they would like to come over to his tree!

Do snakes dance with each other?

After their long winter sleep, snakes shake themselves and slither around in the warmth of spring. Several males gather around one female, who is bigger than they are. The males sway and hiss and try to twine around her in a loving dance. The female chooses the healthiest, and most persistent, male as her mate.

Can animals sing under the water?

Moans, grunts, and squeals drift through the waters of the world's oceans. They are the cries of whales singing for mates. Male humpback whales sing to tell female humpbacks that they are nearby and available to be fathers. The males also slap their flippers and tails on to the surface of the water. This must be the world's slowest, heaviest courtship dance!

The Indian peacock, with its beautiful feathers, has a very loud cry. This bird's noisy screech can be heard from several miles away.

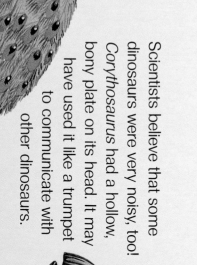

Scientists believe that some dinosaurs were very noisy, too! *Corythosaurus* had a hollow, bony plate on its head. It may have used it like a trumpet to communicate with other dinosaurs.

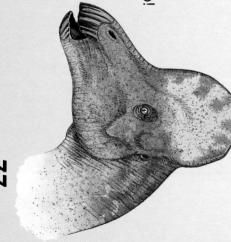

77

Dinosaur Weapons

Fossil remains show that many dinosaurs were armed with deadly weapons. They used these to attack each other or to defend themselves. A dinosaur's weapons were parts of its body—its teeth, horns, claws, or tail. Meat-eating dinosaurs were built to kill. They attacked their victims with sharp teeth and slashing claws. Some plant-eating dinosaurs had weapons to defend themselves against these hunters or perhaps to fight rival males. They used horns, clublike tails, or armor plating to defeat their attackers.

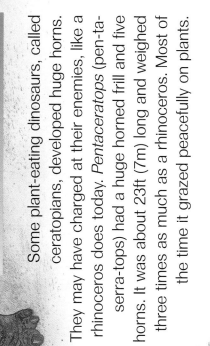

Did dinosaurs have horns?

Some plant-eating dinosaurs, called ceratopians, developed huge horns. They may have charged at their enemies, like a rhinoceros does today. *Pentaceratops* (pen-ta-serra-tops) had a huge horned frill and five horns. It was about 23ft (7m) long and weighed three times as much as a rhinoceros. Most of the time it grazed peacefully on plants.

Which dinosaur had a club?

The armored dinosaur *Euoplocephalus* (you-oh-plo-sef-al-us) had a deadly club on its tail. If attacked, this well-defended plant-eater may have turned around and swiped its enemy with its heavy tail-club.

How do scientists reconstruct dinosaurs?

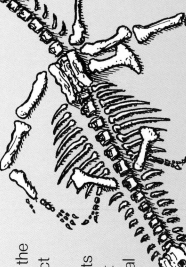

When fossils are first dug up, they are just a jumble of bones. Horns, claws, and neck and tail bones are mixed up with ribs and leg bones. Often there are bones missing.

1. Scientists lay out the bones in their correct order. If a bone is missing, the scientists make a replacement from a tough material called fiberglass.

78

Could dinosaurs kill with their claws?

Many dinosaurs had claws. Deinonychus (dy-non-i-kus) had a very large, killing claw on the second toe of each back foot. This small, swift hunter probably ran and leaped on its victim and slashed with its claws.

Why did Diplodocus have thumb spikes?

No one knows for sure, but it may have used them as weapons. Diplodocus (dip-lo-doh-cus) was huge. It was as heavy as two elephants and as long as a tennis court. Few predators would attack such a large beast. But, if a carnosaur like Allosaurus (al-oh-saw-rus) did attack, Diplodocus fought back. It probably lashed its enemy with its tail and jabbed it with its thumb spikes.

Which dinosaur wore spikes and shields?

Some armored dinosaurs, such as Edmontonia (ed-mon-toh-nee-ah), were built like tanks. Its body was covered with thick, bony shields. Sharp spikes on its shoulders and down the sides of its body gave greater protection. The only place a predator could hurt this dinosaur was in its soft underbelly.

2. An engineer makes a steel frame, called an armature. The leg bones are then rested on the armature. The rest of the bones are slowly added to build the dinosaur.

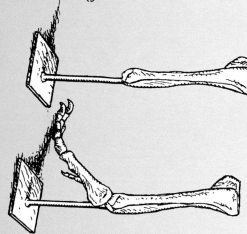

3. The tail and skull are added last, completing the dinosaur skeleton. Bones can also be hung from a ceiling by steel wires instead of being rested on a support.

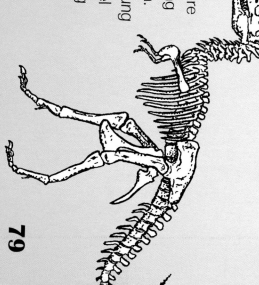

Staying Healthy

When animals get ill and hurt themselves they can't go to a doctor or a dentist. Instead, animals have to look after themselves. They know by instinct what to do. Sometimes they may eat or drink something that works like a kind of medicine, or they may lick and clean a wound. Animals know that when they are ill or injured they have to lie quietly and rest to help themselves get better as quickly as possible.

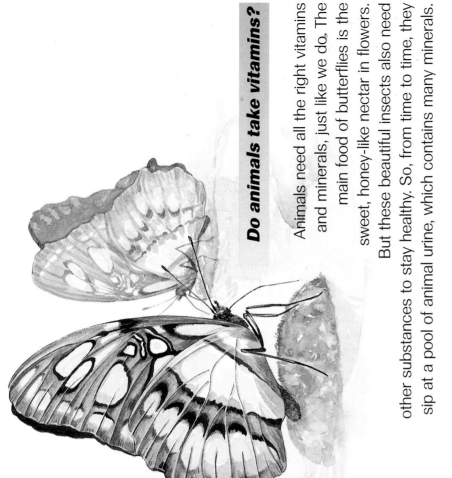

Do animals take vitamins?

Animals need all the right vitamins and minerals, just like we do. The main food of butterflies is the sweet, honey-like nectar in flowers. But these beautiful insects also need other substances to stay healthy. So, from time to time, they sip at a pool of animal urine, which contains many minerals.

Do animals wear plasters?

Even a small cut can be very dangerous for a hippopotamus. Hippos live in muddy rivers, so if a cut is not covered up and the water is dirty, the injury can become infected and never heal. To avoid this, the hippo rolls in wet earth to cover and protect the wound. Its plaster is made of mud!

Which are the most venomous animals?

Many snakes are harmless but others have powerful venoms. The fierce snake is one of the most venomous land snakes of all. Luckily it is not a very common snake and it is quite shy.

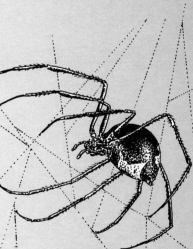

Nearly all spiders use venom to protect themselves or kill their prey. The redback spider's venom is very powerful and can be dangerous to people.

80

Why do parrots eat rocks?

Macaws and other parrots are tropical birds that eat leaves, fruits, nuts, and seeds. Some also feed on small animals, such as insects and worms. If they don't eat enough different foods, they become ill. Then macaws prescribe their own medicine. They fly to special, soft rocks that are full of minerals. There, they scrape the rocks with their beaks and eat the mineral-rich rock dust.

Do animals ever go to the dentist?

Big fish sometimes get bits of food left in their mouths and blood-sucking pests can become attached to their skin and scales. Instead of visiting a dentist or doctor, a small fish, called a cleaner wrasse, nibbles away the old food and pests for them. The wrasses even clean inside the fishes' mouths. The bigger fish could easily eat the cleaner wrasses, but they never do.

Why do dogs sometimes eat grass?

Dogs like to munch meat and crack bones, but if they start to feel sick they may eat grass. Then they are sick and this clears any bad or rotten food from their stomachs. The dog's wild cousin, the wolf, does exactly the same thing.

The box jellyfish, also called the double sea wasp, is one of the most venomous creatures in the world. This animal can have as many as 60 stinging tentacles, each up to 15ft (4.5m) long.

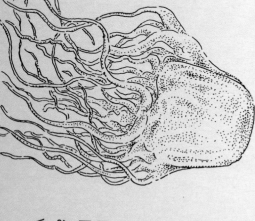

The blue-ringed octopus only measures up to 8 inches (20cm) from one tentacle tip to another. This pretty little octopus, with its bright blue markings, actually has a highly venomous bite.

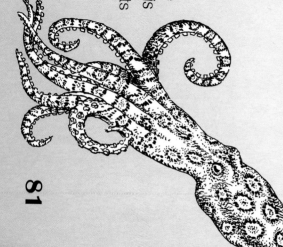

81

Social Bugs

Some creepy crawlies, such as termites, ants, and bees, live together in large groups called colonies. All the animals in the group help one another collect food, find shelter, and fight enemies. This helps the whole group survive. Insects that live in colonies are called social insects. Bugs that don't usually live in groups sometimes gather together for other reasons. This may be to mate, or at a good feeding place. They will soon go off on their own again.

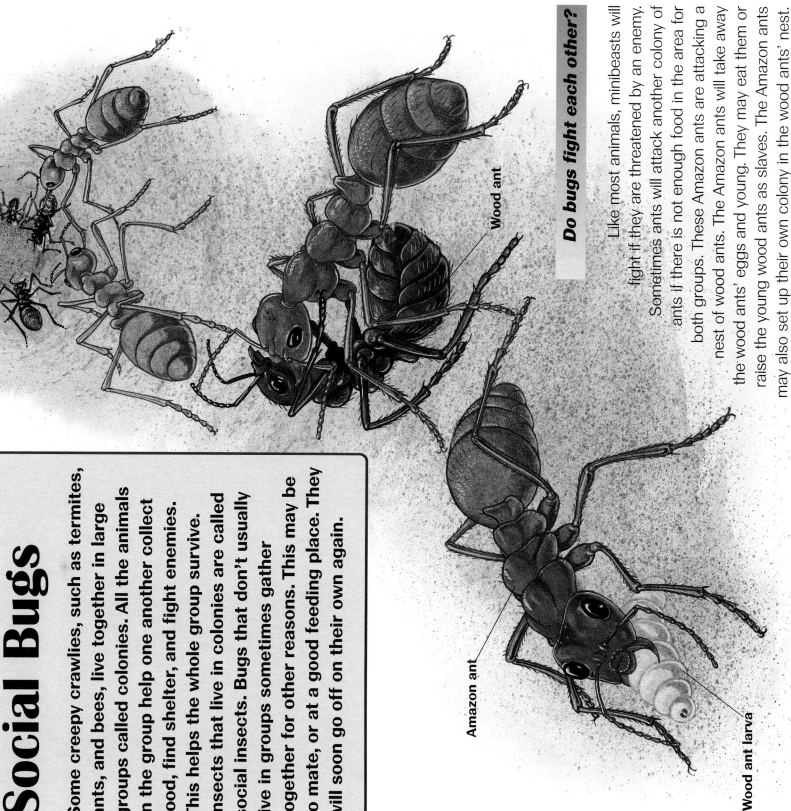

Amazon ant

Wood ant larva

Wood ant

Do bugs fight each other?

Like most animals, minibeasts will fight if they are threatened by an enemy. Sometimes ants will attack another colony of ants if there is not enough food in the area for both groups. These Amazon ants are attacking a nest of wood ants. The Amazon ants will take away the wood ants' eggs and young. They may eat them or raise the young wood ants as slaves. The Amazon ants may also set up their own colony in the wood ants' nest.

Why do bees dance?

1. A honeybee dances to tell other bees where she has found food. If the food is within 160ft (50m), the scout bee dances in a circle, then turns and circles in the other direction.

2. When flowers are farther away, the scout dances a figure eight. Facing downward on the honeycomb means the food is on the other side of the hive from the sun.

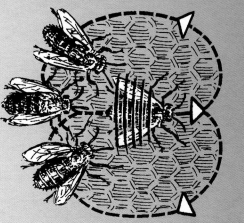

How many bees live in a nest?

Bees' nests vary in size depending on the kind of bee. Honeybees live together in large nests of up to 50,000 bees. There are three types of honeybee, all with different jobs in the hive. The queen bee spends her time laying eggs—up to 1,500 a day. Worker bees look after the hive, the queen, and the young. They also gather nectar and make honey. Males, called drones, mate with the queen. Beekeepers build special hives for honeybees so they can remove the honey easily.

Do some bees live alone?

Many kinds of bees and wasps live on their own. They build small nests in the ground or in hollow plant stems. The female potter wasp mixes sand and mud with her saliva to make a vase-shaped nest. She stings a caterpillar to paralyze it and puts it in the nest. Then she lays her eggs on the caterpillar. Her larvae will have a ready-made meal when they hatch.

Why do bugs gather in one place?

Most minibeasts, such as these woodlice, live on their own. They gather together by chance because they live in the same kinds of places. Woodlice need to live in damp places, such as under leaves or the bark of a tree. They must not dry out, or they will die. That is why you often find several living in the same damp place.

3. If the flowers are between the sun and the hive, the scout dances up the hive wall. Dancing in a straight line slowly means the food is far away. If she moves fast, the food is nearby.

4. If the food is to the left or right of the hive, the bee dances at an angle in the same direction. The angle she dances tells the workers the angle between the flowers and the sun.

Death of the Dinosaurs

Dinosaurs lived on Earth for over 160 million years. They first appeared about 230 million years ago. The last dinosaurs roamed the world 65 million years ago. Then all dinosaurs died out—they became extinct. Experts believe that they disappeared gradually in some areas and more suddenly in others. Dinosaurs were not the only living things to disappear. Many other animals and plants died out at the same time. The reasons for this mass extinction are not known. Scientists have come up with many theories.

Did dinosaurs starve to death?

Albertosaurus (al-ber-toh-saw-rus) was one of the last dinosaurs. This large carnosaur was similar to *Tyrannosaurus rex* (ty-ran-oh-saw-rus reks). Did these huge creatures die out from lack of suitable food? Or did they die from disease? Their death may have been caused by more than one thing. Perhaps we shall never know.

Did dinosaurs freeze to death?

Triceratops (try-serra-tops) lived at the end of the Age of Dinosaurs. The climate began to change at about this time. The tropical climate of North America became cooler and more seasonal. Perhaps some dinosaurs could not adapt to these changes and could not stand up to the cold. There have been many mass extinctions during the life of Earth. No one is sure why they occur.

When did the dinosaurs live?

Dinosaurs appeared during the Triassic. *Eoraptor* (ee-oh-rap-tor) is the earliest known carnivore.

Dinosaurs, such as the plant-eating *Diplodocus* (dip-lo-doh-cus), appeared in the Jurassic.

Mesozoic Era—The Age of Dinosaurs

Triassic Period: 245–204 million years ago

Jurassic Period: 204–140 million years ago

What do scientists think happened?

Most scientists think that the most likely cause for the death of the dinosaurs was a gigantic rock from space. They have found traces of a huge crater off the coast of Mexico. They think it was caused by a huge chunk of rock, or meteorite, about 6 miles (10km) across, hitting the Earth. This would have thrown up masses of dust and ash. The dust would have formed a huge cloud, blocking out the sun's light and heat. Plants and animals that could not cope with these conditions would have died out.

Tyrannosaurus rex was one of the last dinosaurs to develop in the Cretaceous Period.

With the dinosaurs extinct, the Age of Mammals began with mammals like *Taeniolabis* (ty-nee-oh-lah-bis).

Cenozoic Era—The Age of Mammals

Cretaceous Period: 140–65 million years ago

Tertiary Period: 65–2 million years ago

85

Index